Daughter

You Can
Make It

DAG HEWARD-MILLS

Parchment House

First published by Parchment House 2006
Published by Lux Verbi.BM (Pty) Ltd. 2008
Published by Parchment House 2011
5th Printing 2014

ISBN: 978-9988-596-52-1

Find out more about Dag Heward-Mills at:

Healing Jesus Campaign
Write to: evangelist@daghewardmills.org
Website: www.daghewardmills.org
Facebook: Dag Heward-Mills
Twitter: @EvangelistDag

Dedication
To my wife *Adelaide*, my beloved, my counsellor and partner in ministry. Thank you for loving me just as I am. Thank you for good counsel and good advice. You have been there through the changing scenes of our lives. Thank you for being spiritual and ministry-minded. Thank you for joining me in full-time ministry and helping to build the church. I love you always.

Table of Contents

Foreword

I have had the uncommon privilege of having the author of this book as my husband, pastor, leader, counsellor, lover and friend. He certainly has believed in the callings and giftings of women and the coming into existence of this book accentuates this fact.

The Bible says that while the earth remains, seedtime and harvest, cold and heat, summer and winter, day and night will not cease,(Genesis 8:22). This is indeed a reflection of the lives of the women this book covers. They are women from the different walks of our lives; their issues may very well be our issues too.

A time comes when a woman rises up like Deborah to take up a mantle that should usually be the preserve of a man in order to fill the vacuum created by history and circumstances.

A moment comes when a woman rises up out of obscurity like Esther to save an entire nation and another woman loses her place because she refuses to yield to her husband albeit a drunken one.

This book is more than a mere narrative of the lives of women of the Bible. It has answers for all the questions, usually unspoken, that have resonated from the hearts of many women today. Through these pages we are taught how to see God in the so called 'bane' of a woman, like in childbearing, desiring a husband, or a child, sibling rivalry over man, gynaecological problems and the like.

The book does not merely discuss the challenges of the women of the Bible but mirrors our very lives as women on this planet. It doesn't leave us here; it shows us God's way out. It demonstrates to us the unlimited investment that God has poured into female vessels: our sensitivity to the anointing like the woman with the issue of blood, our God-given perception into the future; not forgetting our role as peacemakers and intercessors as in the case of Abigail of the Bible, our peculiar temptations, "the way of escape" and much more.

In essence, no matter what kind of woman one may be, no matter the challenges, achievements or attributes each one of us possesses, this book is a must-read because it deals with virtually all issues both good and bad. I count myself blessed and privileged to be living in times like these and to be the one to write the foreword for such an enriching, soul-inspiring, comforting and God-directing book. Who knows, Daughters, if we have come to the Kingdom for such a time as this...!!! (Esther4:14).

Thank you Bishop for writing to us, Daughters of the King. Indeed, you truly agree with the Psalmist in Psalm 45:13-15: "the king's daughter is all glorious within; her clothing is woven with gold. She will be led to the king (the most high) in embroidered work; the virgin, her companions, who follow her will be brought to you", (Jehovah)! I trust this book will do just that.

Mrs. Adelaide Heward-Mills

Chapter 1

The Women

This is a book I am writing to women. It is a message for women everywhere. Women were created differently from men and I believe they deserve a special message.

Jesus referred to ladies in two different ways. He would either call them women or daughters.

There is a difference between a daughter and a woman. If I were a lady, I would prefer it if Jesus called me "daughter". I think a daughter is generally more receptive, more open and more humble. In the natural, an adult woman is not as easy to influence as a daughter is.

The Bitterness of Life

Many women are embittered by their lives' experiences. They are hardened, unforgiving and unmerciful. The painful experiences of life have washed away the beauty of faith and trust. "Never trust a man," they say. They say to themselves, "Never trust another woman." I notice how many women live in solitude. They are loners with almost no friends.

Notice how Jesus spoke to the woman of Samaria. He was trying to get this woman to believe the things he was saying.

...WOMAN, BELIEVE ME, the hour cometh, when ye shall neither in this mountain, nor yet at Jerusalem, worship the Father.

John 4:21

Notice how Jesus spoke to the woman caught in adultery. This was a woman who had almost lost her life at the hands of unforgiving men. He wanted her to believe in love again.

3

...WOMAN, WHERE ARE THOSE THINE ACCUSERS? hath no man condemned thee? She said, No man, Lord. And Jesus said unto her, Neither do I condemn thee: go, and sin no more.

John 8:10,11

Notice also how Jesus spoke to this woman who had suffered from scoliosis for eighteen years. This woman had been through many things. She had been in bitterness and pain for a long time. This woman needed a miracle. Notice how Jesus addressed her in church:

...WOMAN, THOU ART LOOSED from thine infirmity. And he laid his hands on her: and immediately she was made straight, and glorified God.

Luke 13:12,13

Chapter 2

The Daughters

Naturally speaking, daughters are not full of bitterness and unforgiveness. There is some sweetness and innocence that characterizes a daughter. Above all, there is a special trust and confidence that a daughter has for her father. Unfortunately, the faith, the hope and the love of daughters fade away as they mature into adult women.

Jesus did refer to some women as daughters. I believe it was because of the faith that they had in him. He noticed the pure love that they had toward him.

Let's look at this group of women whom Jesus ministered to. This time, we notice how he addresses them differently.

In one of the greatest miracles that Jesus ever did, the healing of the woman with the issue of blood, we see Jesus referring to her as a daughter! This woman had been able to tap into the anointing even though others around could not feel anything.

...and she felt in her body that she was healed...
Mark 5:29

And Jesus said, SOMEBODY HATH TOUCHED me: for I perceive that virtue is gone out of me.
Luke 8:46

There is something I want you to notice about this daughter. First of all, she had great trust in Jesus' ability. In her sickness and weakness, she pressed through the crowd until she touched the hem of his garment.

It must have taken great faith for this woman to press through the teeming crowds. That is precisely what made her a great daughter: faith and trust. Her twelve years of bitter experiences with different people were not enough to quench a heart of faith.

Wary Women

Sometimes, a background of sinful experiences with different men makes it difficult for a woman to trust any man. She has little confidence in her father, her pastor or any man of God. She simply cannot believe in the existence of goodness and purity. Sometimes, just by growing up in a culture of suspicion and gossip, the seeds of mistrust are sown forever. Such women tend to be perpetually doubtful, unbelieving, sceptical and suspicious. Typically, a woman who is unable to trust is unable to love. She is full of fear. Perfect love casts out fear. The Bible says love…

…believeth all things…

1 Corinthians 13:7

Daughters Receive the Anointing of Their Fathers

The other outstanding mark about this daughter, (the woman with the issue of blood), was the fact that she received the anointing of Jesus. This is the only record in the Bible of the anointing flowing from one person to another in which both parties literally felt it. Jesus felt the anointing leaving him and the daughter felt the anointing coming into her body.

You see, it is children who receive the most precious gifts from their parents. It is children and not equals or colleagues who receive an inheritance from their fathers.

There comes a time in the life of a woman where she tends to challenge the authority of a man. I do not blame her because many men are irresponsible and untrustworthy.

However, fighting against men and campaigning against their authority may easily keep you from the anointing. You will have a perpetually resistant attitude towards God's gift. You see, many of the vessels that God uses are men.

When you receive someone as a father, you open yourself up to receive the ultimate gift from him. Perhaps, that is why Jesus referred to her as "daughter".

...DAUGHTER, THY FAITH HATH MADE THEE WHOLE; go in peace, and be whole of thy plague.
Mark 5:34

Daughters Are Forever

On another occasion, when Jesus was on his way to the cross, a large crowd of people followed him. In this crowd, there were women who were unhappy about the injustice that was being done to him. They supported him openly and publicly identified with him.

In the hour when all the men and apostles deserted the Lord, the women stood strong. Jesus turned to them and ministered words of prophecy from his heart. He did not refer to these supportive ladies as women, but as daughters.

...DAUGHTERS OF JERUSALEM, weep not for me, but weep for yourselves, and for your children.
Luke 23:28

Decide to be a woman whom Jesus would see as a daughter. Someone who is open to the anointing! Someone who is supportive of the man of God! Someone who is prepared to identify openly and passionately with the vision!

Chapter 3

The Covering

Women Need a Covering

Women need a covering for their lives. This covering serves as a shield of protection. Unfortunately, there are many women who do not acknowledge this reality. They see themselves as equal to men and as good as any one else.

> **But every woman that prayeth or prophesieth with her head uncovered dishonoureth her head...**
> **1 Corinthians 11:5**

It is only with a spirit of humility that you can accept these realities. The Kingdom of God can be pursued best with the attitude of a little child.

> **...Except ye be converted, and BECOME AS LITTLE CHILDREN, ye shall not enter into the kingdom...**
> **Matthew 18:3**

It is important for a woman to be covered spiritually and this covering comes through a head. Whether a woman is married or not, she can have the covering she needs.

> **...the head of the woman is the man...**
> **1 Corinthians 11:3**

This covering is provided sometimes by husbands, pastors or spiritual fathers. A woman ministering without this spiritual covering is out of place. Obviously, if you are married to an unbeliever, he cannot be your spiritual covering.

If you are married to a spiritually dull husband, he is not your covering. Someone who is above you spiritually must provide the covering. That is why it is called a covering.

Dear sister, do you have a spiritual covering? Are you open to the counsel of the men that God has given for your covering? Who is your spiritual covering? Are you a rebel? Do not forget that none of us is above the Word of God.

Chapter 4

Daughter, It's Your Honour!

And Barak said unto her, If thou wilt go with me, then I will go: but if thou wilt not go with me, then I will not go. And she said, I will surely go with thee: notwithstanding the journey that thou takest SHALL NOT BE FOR THINE HONOUR; FOR THE LORD SHALL SELL SISERA INTO THE HAND OF A WOMAN. And Deborah arose, and went with Barak to Kedesh.

Judges 4:8,9

In this story, a woman was given the opportunity to take the honour from a man. A man's job fell into the hands of a woman! Instead of a man rising up to his God-given role of leadership, a woman had to take up the challenge and do his work. This is what is happening in the church today. There are many men who have shirked their responsibilities as leaders and spiritual heads.

Women are doing the things men are supposed to do. And I am happy to say women are doing these jobs very well. There are Deborahs who are ready to take the honour and win battles for the Lord.

I suggest to every pastor, to release the Deborahs into the harvest fields. What the Baraks cannot do, God has raised up Deborahs to do. In my own experience, I have found that women are very good pastors and shepherds. When they get their hands to the plough, things really get moving.

I have found women to be more receptive to the anointing and more open to spiritual leadership. Perhaps the original plan was that men should occupy these great leadership positions. Perhaps in the original plan men should have borne all the fruit. Unfortunately, there are always men like Barak, who for various reasons do not do what they are called to do. This is why God has to fall on people like Deborah to accomplish his will.

Dear friend, the will of God is fixed, settled and unchangeable. God has decided to save this world. Jesus trained twelve disciples (men). I believe that the divine plan is that men should be used to lead the church into victory. However, the reality is that there are men like Barak with us. There must be Deborahs who are going to fill the vacuum created by unfruitful, fearful and indecisive men.

The Scripture tells us that once God's plan is established, he does not turn back his hand. Once he is determined to build his church, he will do it whatever it takes. He has threatened to use stones in the past. If stones can be used, how much more human beings? That's why I believe that women can also be used! Once, a donkey was used to send an important message to a stubborn pastor. Dear friend, if donkeys can be used to preach, so can anyone; and so can women.

If you were drowning and someone threw you a line, you would not ask whether it was a man or a woman who had thrown you the line. Of course, if a man throws you a line, he is more likely to have the strength to pull you out. But when the man does not throw the line, you would be grateful for a line that comes from even a child.

Perhaps this explains why there are so many women in the ministry. There is no need to fight what is already happening. It is better to flow with the reality than to hide your face in the sand and deny it.

Daughter, it is your honour!

Chapter 5

Daughter, It's Your Turn

I believe it is the turn of women to rise up. It is the turn of women to come to the front of the battle. Woman, it is your turn to be a leader!

Men have dominated the field of ministry for many years. Too often, women have been seen as people who cause men of God to fall. But there is far more to a woman than her physical body. It is the turn of women to influence the human race with their spirituality and their anointing. Daughter, it's your turn to be spiritual!

After centuries of being good receivers, it's time for women to give something. Kathryn Khulman introduced the world to the Holy Spirit in a special way. I know of no one who has operated in the healing anointing as Kathryn Khulman did! That is a signal to all women that it is their turn to be anointed. Just like the woman with the issue of blood who received the healing anointing, many women are going to receive the anointing to minister in power. Daughter, it's your turn to be anointed!

I read a prophecy which declared that it is the era of the lioness. God is going to use the woman to bruise the head of the Serpent (Satan) in the last battle.

When we get to Heaven there will be no marriage. There will be no husbands, wives or children. All these things will not matter anymore. What will count is whether you fulfilled your ministry or not! Perhaps you have been seen as an object of a man's pleasure. Today, it's your turn to do something for God in the ministry. Daughter, it is time to rise up in the ministry.

Perhaps you have been kept under by the problems that arise from marriage and childbearing. But this is your hour to emerge in full glory. When a woman takes up a mantle and walks in the wisdom of God she is indestructible! Daughter, it's your turn.

Daughter, it is your honour! This means that it is an opportunity for you to bear fruit for God. It is an opportunity for you to do great things. You can stand side by side with every man, call upon the grace of God and you will do just as well.

This does not mean you are "as good as" in a proud sense. All it means is that you are another Deborah whom God has raised up because the Baraks are too scared, doubtful, uninterested, uncommitted, unwilling and cynical. "To be cynical," means "to be disinclined to recognize or believe in goodness or selflessness".

Daughter, it's your honour! It is your turn! This is a prophetic message to all women. It is the season for women to be fruitful in the ministry. Be humble, be a daughter! The anointing will come upon your life.

Chapter 6

The Temptations of the Daughters

There are many types of women in the world. Some of them have done great things for God and others have brought many problems to this world. A *'woman with direction'*, is a woman who has discovered her real reason for being in this world. The real reason for every woman to be in this world is not to find a husband. Neither is it to bring forth children, per se. Your purpose in this world is to serve the Lord and to do his perfect will. I see you as a woman with direction!

A woman with direction learns from the past. The Bible teaches us that there is nothing new under the sun. Whatever has been in the past is what will happen in the future. No one reading this book should see herself above the mistakes of the past. Your life is just a repetition of someone who has gone on before you.

The thing that hath been, it is that which shall be; and that which is done is that which shall be done: and there is no new thing under the sun. Is there any thing whereof it may be said, See, this is new? it hath been already of old time, which was before us.

Ecclesiastes 1:9,10

The First Woman Was Tempted

And when the woman saw that the tree was good for food, and that it was pleasant to the eyes, and a tree to be desired to make one wise, she took of the fruit thereof, and did eat, and gave also unto her husband with her; and he did eat.

Genesis 3:6

Many things can be said about Eve. She was the one who was tempted. Today many women are tempted. Eve was tempted and so will you be tempted. A woman with direction is someone who overcomes temptations. Did you know that a set of distinct

14

temptations exist for women? Every woman must know that there are temptations that are peculiar to women. You see, the temptations of men are different from that of women.

When I became a minister, I was told that ministers are tempted in three main areas: money, sex and fame. Somebody put it this way, "The gold, the girls and the glory."

Tailors are often tempted with the spirit of lying. Doctors are often tempted to have affairs with nurses. Lawyers are often tempted to be immoral.

Daughter, you must understand that there are temptations that are peculiar to you because you are a woman. A woman with wisdom is someone who knows about these temptations. You must be determined to overcome them.

The Temptations of Women

1. The temptation to marry unbelievers

Be ye not unequally yoked together with unbelievers: for what fellowship hath righteousness with unrighteousness? and what communion hath light with darkness?

2 Corinthians 6:14

Many ladies are tempted to marry unbelievers. There are many non-Christian men who come knocking at the doors of young ladies. When no Christian brother is in sight, you are tempted to marry an unbeliever. This is very common. A woman with direction is able to resist this temptation and keep herself.

Many women are tempted to sleep with men. Often ladies sleep with half a dozen or more different men before they eventually settle down. Woman, you will be tempted to do this in order to secure the love of a man. When you go looking for tenderness and love you may receive it, but at a high price. Are you a woman with direction? Then keep yourself pure. Be a woman who overcomes her temptations.

15

2.   The temptation to trust in your beauty

Daughter, do not be taken in by the lies of the devil. Did you think that the devil had stopped whispering lies to women? Certainly not! Demons whisper lies and deception to women all the time. Many women believe that their beauty will last forever. This is why they say "no" to prospective young men when they propose to them.

> **Favour is deceitful, and beauty is vain: but a woman that feareth the LORD, she shall be praised.**
>
> **Proverbs 31:30**

Many women are deceived into thinking that their beauty will charm a man forever.   A woman with direction knows that beauty is vain. She may be beautiful but she is also spiritual.

I have seen a young beautiful girl move in to replace the wife of an older person. If you have seen this before you will know how it usually ends. The younger and more beautiful replacement is also thrown out after a while.

One lady told me that she was going to get somebody's husband. I said to her, "The man is already married." She smiled and said to me, "I am more beautiful than his wife."

Woman, your charm and beauty have an expiration date. They will not last forever. Seek for spiritual things. It is the inner spiritual commitment of the man that makes him faithful to you and not your beauty. Do not believe that beauty is everything.

3.   The temptation to sleep with many people before marriage

Some women are deceived into thinking that if they sleep with a man, he will marry them. Woman, be not deceived! Woman, the man you are currently sleeping with has slept with dozens of other ladies whom he did not marry!

I once read an interesting scientific report about AIDS in Africa. Some people wonder why AIDS is spreading so rapidly in Africa. While AIDS is primarily transmitted through homosexual and bisexual activity in North America and Europe, in Africa, Asia and South America it is primarily transmitted through heterosexual activity (normal male-female relations).

Doctors in the Third World countries confirm that the average sexually active adult in these countries will have between twenty-five and one hundred different sexual partners every year. This level of promiscuity has produced a tragic and widespread epidemic of AIDS. Think about that! Twenty-five to one hundred different partners in one year!

Woman, be not deceived. When a man sleeps with you it means almost nothing. If he can sleep with twenty-five to one hundred people in a year, then you are just an insignificant addition to his list. Woman with direction, do not believe these lies. Do not believe that sex can keep a man attached to you.

4. The temptation to follow material things

Some women have their confidence in material things. This is also a deception. They believe their happiness hinges on having nice carpets, chairs, furniture, cars, clothes, etc. Remember the Word of God! A woman's happiness does not come from the things she possesses.

> **And he said unto them, Take heed, and beware of covetousness: for a man's life consisteth not in the abundance of the things which he possesseth.**
> **Luke 12:15**

5. The temptation to be fearful

> **... whose daughters ye are, as long as ye do well, and are not afraid with any amazement.**
> **1 Peter 3:6**

Perhaps the commonest temptation of women is the temptation to be fearful. The Scripture above teaches that the daughters will do well if they are not afraid.

17

The Common Fears of Women

■　　The fear of not getting married

■　　The fear of not having a child

■　　The fear of marrying the wrong person

■　　The fear of poverty and financial difficulties

■　　The fear of your husband becoming interested in someone else

■　　The fear of your children not doing well

■　　The fear of your husband not loving you anymore

■　　The fear of becoming a widow

■　　The fear of in-laws

■　　The fear of not being liked by others

■　　The fear of being mistreated in the future

■　　The fear of giving your everything and losing it all

■　　The fear of experiencing what you've seen happen to others

■　　The fear of investing your everything into marriage and then losing it all.

Fear is the opposite of faith. Fear influences many women to do the things they do. Humbly analyse your thoughts. See if you are doing what you are doing because of fear. Remember that fear is a demon.

For God hath not given us the spirit of fear; but of power, and of love, and of a sound mind.

2 Timothy 1:7

Fear is not a good reason for marriage. Fear is a demon. A demon should never make you do anything. Fear should never make you criticize and accuse your husband. Do things for the right reasons and God will bless you.

6. The temptation to be emotional

... whose daughters ye are, as long as ye do well, and are not afraid with any amazement.

1 Peter 3:6

"Amazement", speaks of the emotional nature of women. The Scripture teaches that women will do well if they are not amazed (emotional). When the emotions of a woman dominate her, she loses her focus. Emotions can make a woman forget all the Scriptures and principles she knows.

Do not allow emotions of sorrow, fear, jealousy, hatred, and insecurity to overwhelm you. Remember, you will do well when you are not dominated by your emotions.

7. The temptation to be proud

Because women have suffered greatly from discrimination, they tend to be reactionary. Many women display the pride of a "no-nonsense" person. "I will not take this from any man," they say.

"I will not allow a man to disturb my life. You can't keep me in a cage! Why must I do what you say? I am as good as any man, I can do the job any man can do."

One wife repeatedly told her husband, "I am more intelligent than you are."

There is no need to be proud, there is no need to be reactionary. Humble yourself in the sight of the Lord and he will lift you up! God can promote you better than you can with your words.

8. The temptation to be unforgiving

I often say that women have fish-hook hearts. This is a deep, narrow and retentive heart which stores up all the hurts and experiences of this life. Even non-Christians sing songs that say, "Forgive and forget".

God will not hear your prayers when you do not forgive others. Your life will change dramatically when you learn forgiveness.

Woman, remember that your sins are numerous. It is in your interest to walk in love and to forgive those who have hurt you. This will make you a daughter that pleases the Lord.

Daughter, you can make it. In spite of all these temptations, I see you making it! His grace will see you through.

Chapter 7

The Sins of the Daughters

And when the woman saw that the tree was good for food, and that it was pleasant to the eyes, and a tree to be desired to make one wise, she took of the fruit thereof, and did eat, and gave also unto her husband with her; and he did eat.

Genesis 3:6

1. The sin of disobedience

Many women fall into ugly sins. These are often difficult to talk about or even mention. Woman, you are loosed from the effect of your past mistakes! When you look around you, you may think that you are the only one. The devil's plan is to isolate you and make you depressed.

2. The sin of covetousness

Many women fall prey to the sins of jealousy and covetousness. Woman, accept the blessings that God has given to your neighbour. Do not fight it because you cannot win! Gladly attend the wedding of your friend. As you rejoice with her today, people will rejoice with you one day.

Do not be covetous or think that you must have what everybody else has. Women commonly compare lifestyles and clothes. They want their children to attend certain schools because their neighbour's child does. Woman, be content with your position! When you force yourself to possess things that are not yours you will only turn into a "Jezebel".

3. The sin of being unequally yoked

Be ye not unequally yoked together with unbelievers: for what fellowship hath righteousness with unrighteousness? and what communion hath light with darkness?

2 Corinthians 6:14

Some women disobey God and marry unbelievers. But to marry an unbeliever is not the unpardonable sin. The Church must not drive away people who are married to unbelievers. It does not mean that you must not come to church anymore. The fact that you are married to an unbeliever, does not mean you are not a Christian. You are welcome in the church!

The pastor is not the one married to the unbeliever, you are! So don't be worried. If you have any problems, see your pastor and he will counsel you and pray with you. Woman, the fact that you have made a mistake does not mean you should stay away!

4.   The sin of influencing others to do evil

Woman, thou shall not make thy husband sin. Some women prevent their husbands from going to church. The man is the head, but the woman is surely the neck. Woman, you have a lot of influence. Use it wisely! Do not use your influence to make your husband stay away from God.

The Woman Who Made Her Husband Sin

I remember a woman whose husband was willing to donate some money to the church for some instruments. When the man raised up his hand, the woman pulled it down. She stopped him from giving to the Lord. She came up later to lie to the pastors about how stingy the husband was. Woman, do not make your husband sin.

Eve was the woman who made her husband fall into sin.

...and gave also unto her husband with her; and he did eat.

Genesis 3:6

Abraham knew how important it was for his son to have the right woman. He knew that she would influence him all the days of his life. He was very specific about whom Isaac could marry.

And Abraham was old, and well stricken in age: and the LORD had blessed Abraham in all things. And

22

Abraham said unto his eldest servant of his house, that ruled over all that he had, Put, I pray thee, thy hand under my thigh: And I will make thee swear by the Lord, the God of heaven, and the God of the earth, that thou shalt not take a wife unto my son of the daughters of the Canaanites, among whom I dwell:

But thou shalt go unto my country, and to my kindred, and take a wife unto my son Isaac.

Genesis 24:1-4

Abraham sent his servant Eliezer to look for a wife for his son Isaac. He knew how important it was to have the right kind of wife. So he went the extra mile to get a good wife for his son. Your role in your husband's life is crucial to the fulfilling of his ministry. You are a very important element in his life. Even if your husband is not saved, you influence him spiritually. Perhaps you are married to an unbeliever, remember what the Scripture says in 1 Corinthians 7:14.

For the unbelieving husband is sanctified by the wife, and the unbelieving wife is sanctified by the husband: else were your children unclean; but now are they holy.

1 Corinthians 7:14

The Bible teaches that the believer sanctifies the unbeliever. Whatever that means, we know that the believing person has a spiritual influence on the unbeliever. This is the reason why Abraham went so far to get a wife for his son.

5. The sin of destroying God's creation

And the Lord God said unto the woman, What is this that thou hast done?...

Genesis 3:13

Through a woman, God's creation was destroyed. God's lovely creation was greatly deformed and destroyed through the pressure created by a wife. In the end, both she and her husband dwelt in the world that she had destroyed. That is why God asked her, "What is this that thou hast done?"

Woman, do not bring a curse on yourself or your loved ones. Please do not do it! If you hunt for somebody else's husband, his wife and children may curse you. If you have a child with someone's husband, you may disrupt a family and even break it up. Woman, do not attract curses into your life.

6.   The sin of idle chatting

Woman, do not gossip and spread bad stories about God's servants. Do not let your gossip and idle chatting destroy people's faith in God's servants. Many women speak about things that they shouldn't speak about.

...they learn to be idle, wandering about from house to house; and not only idle, but tattlers also and busybodies, speaking things which they ought not.

1 Timothy 5:13

7.   The sin of the strange woman

Woman, do anything you can to prevent yourself from becoming a curse. Do not become a strange woman. A strange woman is someone who deliberately goes after men. She hunts them down and has sexual affairs with them. She is a destroyer of churches. She comes with an agenda and carries with her a curse! Are you a stalker? Are you a predator of precious lives?

A strange woman brings down many mighty men of God. There are some ladies who specialize in sleeping with pastors.

For she hath cast down many wounded: yea, many strong men have been slain by her.

Proverbs 7:26

One of my pastors spoke in fear of a lady who had slept with all the pastors in his town. Woman, please do not be a strange woman. Allow God to use you for a good thing and not for evil. Decide never to be a Delilah to anyone! Woman, please do not bring a curse home with you.

Daughter, you can make it. In spite of all these sins, I see you making it! His grace will see you through.

Chapter 8

Daughter, You Made It!

Daughter, Be Beautiful

And the damsel was very fair to look upon, a virgin, neither had any man known her: and she went down to the well, and filled her pitcher, and came up.

Genesis 24:16

Rebekah was a beautiful woman. There is no woman on this Earth who has not been created in beauty and glory. "Beauty lies in the eyes of the beholder", they say. As you read this book, I wish to inform you that you are beautiful! If you believe this, then it will help you to know how powerful you are.

But Rebekah did not allow her beauty to lead her into sin. A virtuous woman may be beautiful but will not yield to the many overtures that are made by men.

The virtuous woman is a beautiful virgin. She is a beauty and at the same time she is holy. Can you be beautiful and wait for your marriage? Notice what the Bible says in Genesis 24:16. She was beautiful, yet no man had had anything to do with her.

Daughter, Be Homely

...and she went down to the well, and filled her pitcher, and came up.

Genesis 24:16

Rebekah was involved in practical housework. Many beautiful women are just concerned about their hair, their nails and their dresses. Because of this, they are of no practical use in their homes. They cannot cook nor do homely things. Are you just a beautiful woman?

Did you know that the power of physical beauty does not last very long? Rebekah was a woman who was kind. She was a virtuous woman. She spoke respectfully to the servant Eliezer.

And she said, Drink, my lord: and she hasted, and let down her pitcher upon her hand, and gave him drink.
Genesis 24:18

Notice how Rebekah refers to Eliezer as lord. The virtuous woman is someone who has good manners and is respectful. Daughter, there is no need to be angry at your servants everyday. There is no need to rave and rant around the house. Treat your servants with respect and God will bless you for that. Always remember that you could have been that servant. You could have been on the other side of the fence.

Daughter, Be Hospitable

Rebekah was very hospitable.

She said moreover unto him, We have both straw and provender enough, and room to lodge in.
Genesis 24:25

She did not mind having guests. In fact, she welcomed guests. A virtuous woman is someone who welcomes guests and treats them nicely. Think of how you would like to be treated if you were a guest in somebody's home.

Daughter, You Must Decide

And they called Rebekah, and said unto her, Wilt thou go with this man? And she said, I will go.
Genesis 24:58

Many women cannot make decisions. They are ruled by their emotions and their feelings. Because of this, they are left out of the blessings of God. Daughter, God did not give you only feelings. He did not only give you a heart. He gave you a mind.

26

Rebekah was asked whether she would marry Isaac. She had not even seen him before. Some people think that she had no part in the decision that was taken. But as you see in the Scripture above, she had to decide whether she would go or not! She based her decision on facts and wisdom. She married a good man and God blessed her. Sometimes you must allow your mind to lead the way and let your heart follow later.

Daughter, there are not always many suitors available. When God brings a blessing to you, do not discard it with flimsy reasons. It may be your one and only chance to be married. Seek good counsel. Use your mind and be a woman with direction. Daughter, make a decision and God will bless you.

And Isaac brought her into his mother Sarah's tent, and took Rebekah, and she became his wife; and he loved her: and Isaac was comforted after his mother's death.

Genesis 24:67

When Rebekah eventually met with her husband, the Bible says she became his wife. She rose to the occasion and became a happy wife. She became a famous woman and a queen because she was a wise decision-maker. There are two types of women in this world: women who make wise decisions and women who make emotional decisions. When you are a woman who makes wise decisions you will become the envy of all other women.

Daughter, Be Modest

...therefore she took a vail, and covered herself.

Genesis 24:65

When Rebekah met up with her future husband, she covered herself decently. She knew that she was not yet married. It was not yet time to expose herself. A virtuous woman covers herself decently with appropriate clothing.

Woman, cover yourself when necessary. Do not expose what must not be exposed. Perhaps you think you are being

27

fashionable by exposing your body. Much of the fashion of this world is designed by the devil himself. It is designed to promote a culture of immorality and licentiousness.

If you follow what the world is doing, you will often end up in sin. Please read the following verse and see for yourself. The prince of the air is directing the course of the world.

Wherein time past ye walked according to the course of this world, according to the prince of the power of the air, the spirit that now worketh in the children of disobedience:

Ephesians 2:2

Daughter You Can Make It!

And Esau was forty years old when he took to wife Judith the daughter of Beeri the Hittite, and Bashemath the daughter of Elon the Hittite: Which were a grief of mind unto Isaac and to Rebekah.

Genesis 26:34, 35

No woman is exempt from the host of family problems that arise. Rebekah had a son who caused her much grief. A virtuous woman will also have problems.

God did not promise us a bed of roses. But he promised to help us and lift us up. Woman, do not be discouraged because you face problems.

There is nothing new under the sun. You are not the first woman to be beaten by your husband, and you will not be the last. Woman, you are not the only woman whose husband is unfaithful. Woman, you are not the only one whose husband is not saved. Woman, you are not the only one who is not married. Rise up with the Word of God and use your spiritual weapons to overcome every attack of the enemy.

Listen to tapes everyday and your faith will be built up. Faith comes by hearing and hearing by the Word of God. Faith is the

28

shield that quenches all darts thrown against your life. The more
faith you have, the bigger your shield of defence will be.

**Above all, taking the shield of faith, wherewith ye shall
be able to quench all the fiery darts of the wicked.**

Ephesians 6:16

Daughter, Don't Be Biased

**And Rebekah heard when Isaac spake to Esau his
son. And Esau went to the field to hunt for venison,
and to bring it. And Rebekah spake unto Jacob her
son, saying, Behold, I heard thy father speak unto Esau
thy brother, saying, Bring me venison, and make me
savoury meat, that I may eat, and bless thee before the
Lord before my death.**

**Now therefore, my son, obey my voice according to
that which I command thee. Go now to the flock, and
fetch me from thence two good kids of the goats; and
I will make them savoury meat for thy father, such as
he loveth: And thou shalt bring it to thy father, that he
may eat, and that he may bless thee before his death.**

Genesis 27:5-10

Rebekah obviously had her favourite; she preferred Jacob to
Esau. When Isaac wanted to bless his firstborn son, Rebekah was
not happy that her favourite was being left out. She manipulated
events so that Jacob could have a greater blessing.

The Bible teaches us that it is not wise to be partial or
hypocritical. Many parents do not know that children can see
through these things. Partiality stirs up much hatred.

**But the wisdom that is from above is first pure, then
peaceable, gentle, and easy to be intreated, full of
mercy and good fruits, without partiality, and without
hypocrisy.**

James 3:17

Daughter be wise! Govern your home with fairness and
equity.

Daughter, Do Not Interfere

Rebekah interfered with the plan of God Almighty. God has laid down his Words with a special blessing for the firstborn. However, through the interference of Rebekah, God's plan concerning the firstborn did not materialize.

There are women who interfere with the ministry of the Lord Jesus. I want you to know that this only brings a curse upon your life. Rebekah knew that she was inviting a curse upon her life and her son's life. That is why she told her son, "Do not worry, I will receive the curse for you."

And his mother said unto him, Upon me be thy curse, my son: only obey my voice, and go fetch me them.
Genesis 27:13

Perhaps your husband is destined to be a great man of God. Allow the plan of God to come to pass. Perhaps God is going to use you to do great things for him. Allow the plan of God to happen. Perhaps God wants you and your family to join a particular church, do not allow pride to keep you away. Do not interfere with God's plan for your life. Let your children be godly and spiritual.

Daughter, Maintain Good Relationships

Rebekah was no longer living with her family. She had a brother called Laban.

And Rebekah had a brother, and his name was Laban: and Laban ran out unto the man, unto the well.
Genesis 24:29

Even though she had not seen her brother for many years, she kept a good relationship with him. Even though there was great distance between them, she maintained a healthy relationship. Woman, do not disrupt the relationships that God has given to you.

Some women tend to quarrel with people all the time. They are not able to keep relationships for a long time. But a virtuous woman is able to maintain every relationship that God gives to her.

Several years later, Rebekah needed someone she could send her son to for protection. She remembered that she had a brother somewhere and she sent Jacob to him.

Now therefore, my son, obey my voice; and arise, flee thou to Laban my brother to Haran; And tarry with him a few days, until thy brother's fury turn away; Until thy brother's anger turn away from thee, and he forget that which thou hast done to him: then I will send, and fetch thee from thence: why should I be deprived also of you both in one day?

Genesis 27:43-45

Perhaps one day you will need the help of an old friend. Perhaps one day you will need to come back to the same pastor for help. Be careful with the good relationships that God gives you. Be a woman who prevents quarrels and conflicts.

A virtuous woman is someone who brings peace.

Daughter, Don't Kill Yourself

And Rebekah said to Isaac, I am weary of my life because of the daughters of Heth: if Jacob take a wife of the daughters of Heth, such as these which are of the daughters of the land, what good shall my life do me?

Genesis 27:46

Woman, please do not kill yourself with your confessions. There are many things that are happening that do not bring joy. Do not allow a spirit of depression to come over you. When you begin to say, "I am weary of my life", you are inviting a spirit of death into your life. Do not allow depression to kill you.

Many things can bring depression. Perhaps you have married a man who has been unfaithful. Perhaps you have discovered

31

other illegitimate children that your husband has. Do not sink into a sea of despair and hopelessness. Remember this, no man can satisfy you so do not expect fulfilment from a man.

You must keep your eyes on the Lord. Do not kill yourself before your time with your own words.

Death and life are in the power of the tongue: and they that love it shall eat the fruit thereof.

Proverbs 18:21

Do not kill your marriage when it is not yet over. Many marriages are destroyed with the tongue. If you curse your marriage, it will be cursed. If you speak life into it, it will revive.

Daughter, do not give up!

Daughter, there is hope in God!

Daughter, I promise you: joy cometh in the morning! After every night, there is day. Everything has an end. There is an expiry date for every problem. The Bible teaches that there is a time for everything. There is a time to start and a time to end. There is a time for trouble but there is also a time for peace.

Your time of peace will surely come!

Daughter, you can make it!

Chapter 9

With All Your Getting, Get Understanding

Wisdom is the principal thing; therefore get wisdom: and with all thy getting get understanding.

Proverbs 4:7

Getting understanding is not the same as getting a breakthrough. It is certainly not an instant solution. But understanding will lead you to the solution. Wisdom is most useful for direction.

When you have wisdom and understanding, you will be a different kind of woman.

Women who give themselves to reading are people of understanding. People who bother to go to university are people of understanding. In the natural, such people have an easier life.

When you thoroughly understand the cause of a problem you are better able to solve it. That is why medical doctors spend so much time trying to diagnose problems. Understanding the problem is often 80% of the solution.

Do you want an easier life? Then get understanding. Make the effort to understand the curse of the Garden of Eden. Understand the root cause of all frustration.

In this book, you will learn about the frustrations of women. You will understand the things that hinder women. Through this understanding you will become a victorious woman.

I cannot say anything greater than the Word of God. Get understanding! Get wisdom!

Chapter 10

Where Frustration Came From

And the Lord God said unto the woman, What is this that thou hast done? And the woman said, The serpent beguiled me, and I did eat. And the Lord God said unto the serpent, Because thou hast done this, thou art cursed above all cattle, and above every beast of the field; upon thy belly shalt thou go, and dust shalt thou eat all the days of thy life: And I will put enmity between thee and the woman, and between thy seed and her seed; it shall bruise thy head, and thou shalt bruise his heel. Unto the woman he said, I will greatly multiply thy sorrow and thy conception; in sorrow thou shalt bring forth children; and thy desire shall be to thy husband, and he shall rule over thee.

Genesis 3:13-16

Women have often been treated as second-class human beings. They have been ridiculed and degraded and used as mere objects of pleasure. I believe that a new day is dawning for the woman who knows God.

A day of promotion and of betterment is coming! Women no longer have to occupy the second place or even the back seat. They must occupy their God-given positions.

There are many frustrations in this world and women are not exempted from them. Every woman will live to fight these battles. But there is a way out of the many frustrations that face women today.

The frustrations of a woman are well described in the curse on Eve in the Garden of Eden. Understanding these problems is the first step to overcoming them.

Always remember that diagnoses solves 80% of your problems. These curses are the most plausible explanation of the state of women.

34

Chapter 11

Seven Hindrances of Women

1. Deception

Women are more susceptible to deception. "Deception" is believing in something that is not true. Many quarrels come about through deception. The Apostle Paul used this point (of the woman often being deceived) to emphasize why they are not to be in leadership.

> **And the LORD God said unto the woman, What is this that thou hast done? And the woman said, The serpent beguiled me, and I did eat.**
>
> **Genesis 3:13**

> **Let the woman learn in silence with all subjection. But I suffer not a woman to teach, nor to usurp authority over the man, but to be in silence. For (because) Adam was first formed, then Eve. And Adam was not deceived, but the woman being deceived was in the transgression.**
>
> **1 Timothy 2:11-14**

The deception of Eve reveals much about the state of women. They more easily believe and they are more easily deceived. Every woman must in humility accept this fact of being more easily deceived. This reality can be confusing since they also easily believe in the right thing.

It is truly amazing that those who more easily receive and believe are also more easily deceived. Many women are more spiritual than their husbands. They believe in God and flow with the Spirit much more quickly. It is difficult to see how such spiritual beings could also be open to deception.

Accepting this reality in humility will attract the grace of God to your life. God will save you from deception and keep you on the path of righteousness.

2.   Satan's enmity for women

Satan hates women. The devil is working to destroy the entire human race, but there is a special hatred he has for women. The Word of God shows us that women are special targets of Satan.

And I will put enmity between thee and the woman, and between thy seed and her seed; it shall bruise thy head, and thou shalt bruise his heel.

Genesis 3:15

This reality explains why women seem to have more problems than men do. They are the special targets of evil spirits. It explains why the plight of women is often so pathetic. It explains the reason for countless women's groups and movements. There is indeed a special onslaught of the enemy on women.

This is why women must be spiritual. Every wise woman will develop herself spiritually. To do this, she must study the Bible, read Christian books and listen to tapes.

3.   The curse of desiring husbands who will dominate them

Many of the problems that women have are related to finding husbands and keeping them. In the church, a large percentage of women's problems are related to this. Marriage, although celebrated in grand style is actually described as a kind of curse in the book of Genesis, chapter three.

...and thy desire shall be to thy husband, and he shall rule over thee.

Genesis 3:16

The desire for husbands is one of the most devastating curses and frustrations unleashed on women. Even the most independent women come to the place where they want a man. Older women, who are unable to give birth anymore, still want to be married. Indeed, a close analysis of the situation will only show the workings of a curse.

This curse is circumvented by the power and the wisdom of God.

4. Multiplied sorrow

...I will greatly multiply thy sorrow and thy conception; in sorrow thou shalt bring forth children...

Genesis 3:16

Women have brought forth the children of this world in sorrow. The huge gynaecological blocks in most hospitals testify to the sorrows of women. The sorrows begin as they try to get pregnant. The sorrows continue through the pregnancy.

Some women lose their health during pregnancy and others lose their beauty. Some die through pregnancy while others permanently lose their attractiveness or even their husbands. The price is high but they pay it over and over, again. After the pregnancy, the struggles and sorrows continue in the bringing up of children.

Through wisdom you will overcome these challenges. The wisdom of medical science has made it possible to have children without so many problems.

5. The sinful nature

The flesh is the carnal nature within every human being. To be carnally minded is death. And he that soweth to the flesh reaps corruption. Many women's lives have been corrupted because they have followed the flesh and the mind. This reality compounds the problems of every woman.

You will never follow your flesh when you understand the Word of God. The power of God will help you overcome the weakness that is in your flesh.

...To be carnally minded is death...

Romans 8:6

6. The weakness

Women are described as the weaker vessels.

...giving honour unto the wife, as unto the weaker vessel...

1 Peter 3:7

A weaker fishing trawler cannot be compared to the might of a nuclear-powered aircraft carrier. The weaker ship is more easily tossed about by every storm or situation. This weakness is the cause of many unplanned emotional excursions by women.

The world of women is characterised by detours of swirling, twirling, weaving and spinning currents of emotions, quarrels and instability. The varied mood swings and temperamental nature of women usually makes them unsuitable for steady leadership.

This is why the Bible is so clear about who is the head in the family and in the church. The Apostle Paul was stronger on this issue than on any other. Paul asserted that if anyone was spiritual, he would acknowledge this reality about women.

Let your women keep silence in the churches: for it is not permitted unto them to speak; but they are commanded to be under obedience, as also saith the law. And if they will learn any thing, let them ask their husbands at home: for it is a shame for women to speak in the church. What? came the word of God out from you? or came it unto you only? If any man think himself to be a prophet, or spiritual, let him acknowledge that the things that I write unto you are the commandments of the Lord.

1 Corinthians 14:34-37

7. The unkindness of men

Generally speaking, men are stronger and more domineering than women. Most men operating from a heart of flesh do not treat women kindly. The wickedness of men operating with the nature of Satan is like the last nail on the coffin.

The need for women's groups which champion women's rights is obvious. Ultimately, it is the Lord who will be the lifter of your head if you are a woman.

Chapter 12

The Woman's Keys

Women do not have to live a life of unhappiness, depression and misery just because of the curse. It is not true that women are hopelessly condemned to a state of unhappiness because of the Adamic curse.

Yes, it is true that the curse explains a lot to us. But there is hope! The good news is that a woman with direction can gain the mastery over the frustrations she finds in this world.

The Keys

There are two keys that make a woman gain the mastery over these difficulties—the power of God and the wisdom of God.

...Christ the power of God, and the wisdom of God.
1 Corinthians 1:24

These two ingredients (power and wisdom) are available to every Christian woman. A woman with direction employs both the power and the wisdom to overcome every arrow that is thrown at her.

The Key of Wisdom

You need wisdom to be a woman with direction. The Bible teaches that wisdom is profitable to direct.

...but wisdom is profitable to direct.
Ecclesiastes 10:10

Many of the problems that confront women cannot be overcome with brute strength. They must be surmounted by the use of wisdom. Unless God intervenes, many of the conditions that face women have no natural solutions. However, the Bible teaches us that wisdom is the key to solving impossible situations.

We can overcome every hopeless situation by the wisdom of God. Read this part carefully!

The Impossible War

The Bible teaches about a city, which faced an impossible war. This was a small town with a few people in it. The town was surrounded by an enemy who set up a great array of armoured vehicles and artillery. Everyone knew that it was just a matter of time before they would all be killed.

But a solution came from an unexpected source. There was a poor wise man who came up with some ideas that delivered the entire city. He did not deliver the city by strength or by any military skills. He delivered the city by wisdom.

There was a little city, and few men within it; and there came a great king against it, and besieged it, and built great bulwarks against it: Now there was found in it a poor wise man, and he by his wisdom delivered the city...

Ecclesiastics 9:14-15

Many women's lives are like that desperate city that faced a hopeless battle. I say this because I am a pastor and I see it all the time. I know that many ladies' lives are like this little town which had no way forward.

Many women are married to men who mistreat them, mishandle them and are unfaithful to them! They live a life of constant quarrelling and unhappiness. It looks as if there is no way forward in their situation. They often have only two options: divorce or a life of misery. Many women just exist in their marriages until they die!

On the other hand, there are many women who desire to marry. Their birthdays are almost like days of mourning. As they grow older, their hope of getting married diminishes.

There are also many women who seek to have children. They try everything, but still there is no child. As the days go by, they become gloomier and gloomier. What can be done about these intractable problems? Today I present you with a fresh ray of hope for your situation.

Wisdom is the way forward. Wisdom is profitable for direction.

... but wisdom is profitable to direct.

Ecclesiastics 10:10

I want you to be a woman with direction. How can you be a woman with direction? The Bible says wisdom is profitable for direction. God will direct you out of every difficult situation.

Just as that man delivered the city from destruction, your entire life is going to be rescued by the wisdom of the Lord.

Wisdom is the principal thing; therefore get wisdom: and with all thy getting get understanding. Exalt her, and she shall promote thee: she shall bring thee to honour, when thou dost embrace her.

Proverbs 4:7, 8

The Scripture we have just read says that we should exalt and embrace wisdom in our lives. 'To embrace', means 'to hold tightly'. I want you to hold tight onto this book until you finish reading it. Then I want you to read it again. I want you to read it until the wisdom that is contained in these pages is transferred into your heart.

The solutions to the multitude of intractable problems that face women are dealt with in the Word of God. A woman with direction is a woman who gets hold of wisdom and doesn't put it down.

How to Get Wisdom

1.   Pray for Wisdom.

If any of you lack wisdom, let him ask of God, that giveth to all men liberally, and upbraideth not; and it shall be given him.

James 1:5

2.   Study the Word.

In him are hidden all the treasures of wisdom and knowledge. The closer you get to God, the more wisdom you will have.

In whom are hid all the treasures of wisdom and knowledge.

Colossians 2:3

The Power

The power of God is the grace of God. God's grace is sufficient for every situation. God will lift you up by His power. There are some things that God wants to do for you. How can you get this grace that you need? The answer is humility. Humble yourself in the sight of the Lord, and He will lift you up.

...for God...giveth grace to the humble.

1 Peter 5:5

Chapter 13

Daughter, While You Wait

While You Wait, Keep Going to Church

And this man went up out of his city yearly to worship and to sacrifice unto the Lord of hosts in Shiloh. And the two sons of Eli, Hophni and Phinehas, the priests of the Lord, were there. And when the time was that Elkanah offered, he gave to Peninnah his wife, and to all her sons and her daughters, portions: But unto Hannah he gave a worthy portion; for he loved Hannah: but the Lord had shut up her womb. And her adversary also provoked her sore, for to make her fret, because the Lord had shut up her womb. And as he did so year by year, when she went up to the house of the Lord, so she provoked her; therefore she wept, and did not eat.

1 Samuel 1:3-7

What does one do while waiting for a miracle? What should you do while you wait for God's answer? Hannah was the woman who kept going to church (Shiloh) in spite of her problems. Hannah is the one from whom we learn what to do while we wait for our miracle!

There are many problems that women face today. A woman with direction is someone who cannot be turned away from her church in spite of her problems. Dear woman, your help comes from God. The devil would like to keep you from the source of your help.

Hannah was suffering from barrenness, and could have stayed at home in her depression. She could have worked all day and night. She could have resorted to witchcraft and all sorts of things to help her. But she kept going to Shiloh. Shiloh is the place where prayers and sacrifices are made to the Lord.

While You Wait, Notice God's Blessings around You

But unto Hannah he gave a worthy portion; for he loved Hannah: but the Lord had shut up her womb. Then said Elkanah her husband to her, Hannah, why weepest thou? and why eatest thou not? and why is thy heart grieved? am not I better to thee than ten sons?

1 Samuel 1:5, 8

Hannah's husband really loved her. The Bible tells us how he gave a worthy portion to her and describes his deep love for her. But Hannah did not notice her husband's love. Hannah wept and wept and did not notice that she had a good husband.

A woman with direction must learn to see beyond her problem. Some women are so taken up with the problems that they cannot see the goodness of God around them. Perhaps there is one fault with your husband. Do not be so taken up with that fault that you don't see how God has blessed you. The grass always seems to be greener on the other side.

At one point, Hannah's husband asked her, "Am I not worth more than ten sons to you?" Perhaps your difficulties have blinded your eyes to the blessings of God. Please do not allow a dark cloud to brood over everything because of the one problem that you have.

Then said Elkanah her husband to her, Hannah, why weepest thou? and why eatest thou not? and why is thy heart grieved? am not I better to thee than ten sons?

1 Samuel 1:8

Hannah could not see that she had a good husband. She could not notice that her husband was very generous and kind. Hannah did not think of the fact that even if she had children they would grow up and leave the home one day. Then she would be all alone with her husband again.

44

Perhaps you are looking for a husband or perhaps you want your husband to be saved. A woman with direction does not allow her problem to overshadow the blessings that she already has. Daughter, while you wait, notice God's blessings! Be thankful for what you have, more is on the way.

While You Wait, Use Your Spiritual Weapons

And she was in bitterness of soul, and prayed unto the Lord, and wept sore.

1 Samuel 1:10

In this verse, you see how Hannah lifted up her eyes to the Lord and prayed with strong cries and tears (Hebrews 5:7). She was a prayer warrior. Daughter, your weapons are not carnal, they are mighty through God. Perhaps you need a baby.

Perhaps you need a husband. Do not resort to physical or human methods to get what you need.

Many problems have spiritual roots and a daughter of destiny knows this! If you are seeking for a baby, it is good to find the appropriate medical care. But a woman with direction knows that prayer is the solution. Keep praying, there is power in prayer. As you study the Bible, you will realize that many people received blessings and breakthroughs through prayer.

Therefore I say unto you, What things soever ye desire, when ye pray, believe that ye receive them, and ye shall have them.

Mark 11:24

Before Hannah could do anything about it, her husband had married someone else in order to have children. This is a very common practice in Africa, since some see the state of not having a child as a curse.

Many husbands are pressurized into finding someone who can have a baby with them. Perhaps, being a second wife is not easy. Even being the only wife is a great challenge. Before Hannah could do anything about it, she was in a bad situation.

Woman, I want you to know that God sees everything you are going through. He is on your side. He will deliver you. He will keep you. I see you being raised out of that impossible situation! As you read this book, a new light is beginning to shine in your life. The days of reproach and humiliation are over. I declare it to be so, in the name of Jesus!

While You Wait, Make a Vow!

And she vowed a vow, and said, O Lord of hosts, if thou wilt indeed look on the affliction of thine handmaid, and remember me, and not forget thine handmaid, but wilt give unto thine handmaid a man child, then I will give him unto the Lord all the days of his life, and there shall no razor come upon his head.

1 Samuel 1:11

Hannah was a woman with direction. She went a step further than many others would. She made a promise to God. If he were to give her a child she would give him back to the Lord. She promised to give away what was most precious to her, even before he was born. Perhaps God is waiting for you to make such a promise to Him. Can you make a vow and keep it?

While You Wait, Keep Your Vows

Hannah kept her vow.

But Hannah went not up; for she said unto her husband, I will not go up until the child be weaned, and then I will bring him, that he may appear before the Lord, and there abide for ever. And Elkanah her husband said unto her, Do what seemeth thee good; tarry until thou have weaned him; only the Lord establish his word. So the woman abode, and gave her son suck until she weaned him.

And when she had weaned him, she took him up with her, with three bullocks, and one ephah of flour, and a bottle of wine, and brought him unto the house of

the Lord in Shiloh: and the child was young. And they slew a bullock, and brought the child to Eli. And she said, Oh my lord, as thy soul liveth, my lord, I am the woman that stood by thee here, praying unto the Lord. For this child I prayed; and the Lord hath given me my petition which I asked of him: Therefore also I have lent him to the Lord; as long as he liveth he shall be lent to the Lord. And he worshipped the Lord there.

1 Samuel 1:22-28

She gave unto the Lord and the Lord gave back to her. Is money a problem to you? Do you find it difficult to give to Jesus? Loose that money and let it go now! Become a "tither" and a giver of offerings.

A woman with direction is someone who pays her first and best fruits or tithes to the Lord. She makes a vow that she is going to support the ministry and she sticks to her word.

There are many women who have a problem with money. Woman, do not let the god of this world have any control of your life. There are many blessings that are released when you pay your vows.

Do you know that when Abraham gave tithes to the Lord, the blessing he received was a child? The Bible teaches us that Abraham was very rich, he didn't need anymore money. God knows what you need. As you give to him, God will give you what you need.

Principles are things that happen whether you want them to or not! There is a principle about giving. The more you give the more you receive.

Give, and it shall be given unto you; good measure, pressed down, and shaken together, and running over, shall men give into your bosom. For with the same measure that ye mete withal it shall be measured to you again.

Luke 6:38

47

Hannah gave one son to the Lord—the principle worked! God gave her five more children in return.

Help Your Son to Become a Pastor!

Moreover his mother made him a little coat, and brought it to him from year to year, when she came up with her husband to offer the yearly sacrifice.

1 Samuel 2:19

In this Scripture, you will notice how Hannah gave her son for the ministry. She knew that his life was going to be different from other little children. It was a great sacrifice for her to bring her only child to the temple. She knew his life was going to be difficult. Nevertheless, she kept her promise and gave up what was valuable to her.

Make a Preacher's Coat for Your Son

Then she made him a little coat to help him in the ministry. That little coat represents her contribution to his ministry. She was giving him clothes that he could use in church.

A woman with direction is somebody who would like her child to serve the Lord. Some people do not want their husbands or children to go anywhere near the ministry. They have a subtle way of opposing the thought of becoming ministers. A woman with direction will release her husband or her child to the ministry. Daughter, help your husband to fulfil his calling.

Daughter, Keep on Singing

Hannah was a woman who wrote and sang songs after she had children. Many Christians today leave the music ministry after they have had children. They no longer praise the Lord as they used to. Hannah composed beautiful songs. She composed "There is none holy as the Lord."

After her promotion, she was found in the house of the Lord praying. She could still be found singing. Many women desire a breakthrough from the Lord, but when they receive it, they complain about how busy they are with their children. They explain how they are suffering from morning sickness. They can no longer be in church because of backaches.

Thank God for spiritual daughters! A woman with direction stays with the Lord even after the blessing has come. A woman with direction becomes even more zealous after the promotion of God.

Woman, Can You Be Separated from Your Child?

Some women are so attached to their children that they are of no use to anyone! Their husbands suffer because a child has come. The church suffers because a child has come. Sometimes their work suffers as well.

A woman with direction is not overwhelmed because of a child. She does not allow her child to separate her from the will of God. She is able to leave her child for a few hours so that she can fulfil her ministry. Woman, do not be overwhelmed by the blessing of childbirth.

Woman, Go beyond Your Emotions

And as he did so year by year, when she went up to the house of the Lord, so she provoked her; therefore she wept, and did not eat. Then said Elkanah her husband to her, Hannah, why weepest thou? and why eatest thou not? and why is thy heart grieved? am not I better to thee than ten sons?

1 Samuel 1:7,8

Hannah was an emotional person. You can see in the Scriptures that she wept and cried like any other woman. She had feelings and emotional problems. But she went beyond her emotions and became a spiritual person. In fact, she became more spiritual after her problem.

Daughter, allow God to draw you deeper into the things of the Spirit. Through your problems, you will get to know God better. Indeed, all things will work out for your good. Woman, there is a breakthrough waiting for you. Go beyond your emotions and become a spiritual person.

Chapter 14

Daughter, Catch the Anointing

And when Jesus was passed over again by ship unto the other side, much people gathered unto him: and he was nigh unto the sea. And, behold, there cometh one of the rulers of the synagogue, Jairus by name; and when he saw him, he fell at his feet, And besought him greatly, saying, My little daughter lieth at the point of death: I pray thee, come and lay thy hands on her, that she may be healed; and she shall live. And Jesus went with him; and much people followed him, and thronged him.

And a certain woman, which had an issue of blood twelve years, And had suffered many things of many physicians, and had spent all that she had, and was nothing bettered, but rather grew worse, When she had heard of Jesus, came in the press behind, and touched his garment. For she said, If I may touch but his clothes, I shall be whole. And straightway the fountain of her blood was dried up; and she felt in her body that she was healed of that plague.

And Jesus, immediately knowing in himself that virtue had gone out of him, turned him about in the press, and said, Who touched my clothes? And his disciples said unto him, Thou seest the multitude thronging thee, and sayest thou, Who touched me? And he looked round about to see her that had done this thing.

But the woman fearing and trembling, knowing what was done in her, came and fell down before him, and told him all the truth. And he said unto her, Daughter, thy faith hath made thee whole; go in peace, and be whole of thy plague.

Mark 5:30-31

51

Daughters Are Receptive

I am a firm believer in the ability of women to catch the anointing. Many people brand women as being emotional. With the passage of years, I think I can say that women are more receptive to the Holy Spirit than men. This receptivity is often misunderstood.

Dear sister, the anointing is yours for the taking. You must reach out with your spirit and take what God has for you. Do not be intimidated any longer by the brothers who are stiff and unyielding to the Holy Spirit. There is a difference between a man and a woman. I have noticed that difference when it comes to the things of the Lord.

If you look closely at the story of the woman with the issue of blood, you will learn certain things about women catching the anointing. Jesus was surrounded by his disciples.

On that day in particular, the anointing was flowing at a very high level. A few hours earlier, Jesus had cast out six thousand demons from a mad man in Gadara. He had crossed the river and was on his way to raise the dead.

The twelve disciples were very close to the anointing but did not have what it took to connect to the power. A certain smelly, nameless woman (unnamed up till today) came up to Jesus. She had what it took to connect to the anointing that was on Jesus.

As soon as she touched the hem of Jesus' garment, something happened to her. The anointing passed into her. Jesus felt it and she did as well.

And Jesus, immediately knowing in himself that virtue had gone out of him, turned him about in the press, and said, Who touched my clothes?

Mark 5:30

When Jesus asked his disciples who had tapped into the anointing, they were very surprised. They asked the Lord, "What are you talking about?" They stuttered, "Which power is flowing where?" They were confused and they asked one another, "What is he talking about? I don't feel anything, do you?" They turned on Jesus, defending their insensitivity to the things of the Spirit.

They said to him, "Can't you see that the masses are jostling you? What you felt was not the anointing. You were just feeling the pressure of the crowds surrounding us. It seems that you are becoming emotional." Merzee!*

But Jesus knew that the anointing was flowing. He also knew that somebody had received it. The nameless woman in the crowd had already begun to rejoice because she had received the power.

And straightway the fountain of her blood was dried up; and she felt in her body that she was healed of that plague.

Mark 5:29

Is it not amazing that the disciples did not recognize or feel the flow of the Spirit in the service? An unidentified person from nowhere came up and received it all. This is a common pattern I have noticed.

Sometimes, when I pray for people at the altar, I notice that the women are more receptive. They feel the power of God. They sense the Spirit moving. Sometimes, the men are like marble statues covered with plaster of Paris. Some people cannot receive anything. You see, the power of God can be felt. Jesus felt it going out of him. The woman with the issue of blood also felt the power coming into her. You may see all these things as emotionalism. I can assure you that there is more to it than the emotions of a woman. Daughter you are receptive.

---

* The expression "Merzee" is the author's colloquial exclamation.

Sometimes women become intimidated by the people around them. They feel that they are being hysterical. Daughter, you are not hysterical. You are just receptive to the Spirit of God! However, you will notice that there seem to be more men actively involved in ministry. Why is this? There are a few reasons why more men come into ministry. You will notice that this woman with the issue of blood never became a minister. If she did, it is not mentioned in the Bible.

However, we see the disciples becoming successful apostles, prophets, and teachers. In the second chapter of Acts, we see the disciples receiving the anointing and speaking in tongues. It took them longer to receive the anointing. But when they did, the results were dramatic. We watched them become ministers in the book of Acts. I believe that women receive the anointing far quicker than men do, but the cares of this world choke the Word and it becomes unfruitful.

And the cares of this world, and the deceitfulness of riches, and the lusts of other things entering in, choke the word, and it becometh unfruitful.

Mark 4:19

There are three areas where women are particularly affected. First of all, in the area of finding husbands. Secondly, ensuring that their marriages are successful and peaceful. And thirdly, the bearing and raising of children. I have watched women with great anointing lose their ministry as they succumbed to these realities.

Woman, through no fault of yours, you will have to grapple with these realities. It is only if you are determined that you will remain in ministry.

In my church, I have found that women are very good shepherds and pastors. Some of my best pastors are women. When they are able to overcome these three challenges, they become extremely useful. Daughter, you received the anointing. You must prevail with the anointing.

Daughter, Take These Steps

Daughter, it is important to study the steps that this unnamed woman took as she came to the anointing. You must study closely what this unnamed woman did in order to receive from God. God has many things in store for you. Notice the four steps that this woman took to receive the anointing. I learnt these steps from Kenneth Hagin.

Step number one, she heard it.

Step number two, she believed it.

Step number three, she said it.

Step number four, she did it.

She Heard It!

When she had heard of Jesus, came in the press behind, and touched his garment.

Mark 5:27

A daughter of destiny must expose herself to the Word of God so that she will hear the right things. The more you hear, the more you believe. The more you believe, the more you are open to the blessings of God. Woman with direction, are you someone who listens to tapes? Do you watch videos? Do you read books? Or are you just seeking after blessings?

She Believed It!

This woman did certain things that brought her a certain blessing. She believed. The more you hear, the more you will believe. I want you to believe that God has answered your prayers. I want you to believe that you will prosper. It is more beneficial for you to believe than to doubt. Believe that God has given you a good husband and a good marriage. Do not doubt it, no matter your age.

She Said It!

Thirdly, this woman said it. I want you to say positive things from today. Speak positively. You are anointed. Speak positively. With the heart you believe and with the mouth confession is made unto salvation. You must make positive confessions about your life. For practical help on making positive confessions, see Bishop Heward-Mills' book, "Name It! Claim It! and Take It."

She Did It!

The fourth and final step is to do something. Stretch out your heart and hand and receive from the Lord. If you want a husband, do something about it. After hearing and believing that God is going to bless you, dress nicely, look smart and be friendly. Everybody wants to marry someone who is warm and has feelings. Daughter, never forget these four steps to your blessing. Hear it, believe it, say it and do it!

Chapter 15

Daughter, Is There a Curse Somewhere?

...so that things which are seen were not made of things which do appear.

Hebrews 11:3

Everything you see in the physical or natural world is a reflection of a spiritual reality. It is the spiritual that gives rise to the physical.

To understand the way forward you need to know where you are spiritually. If you do not know where you are, you don't even know whether to turn left or right. Perhaps you are in the north or the south.

Which way do you turn? You will only know which way to turn by knowing where you are. In order to understand the state of women, you have to understand where women are, spiritually speaking.

The main thing that defines the spiritual state of women is the curse that took place in the Garden of Eden.

Unto the woman he said, I will greatly multiply thy sorrow and thy conception; in sorrow thou shalt bring forth children; and thy desire shall be to thy husband, and he shall rule over thee.

Genesis 3:16

Every woman falls squarely under the influence of this curse. When you study this curse thoughtfully, you will realize that no woman is exempted.

And I will put enmity between thee and the woman, and between thy seed and her seed; it shall bruise thy head, and thou shalt bruise his heel. Unto the woman he said, I will greatly multiply thy sorrow and thy

conception; in sorrow thou shalt bring forth children; and thy desire shall be to thy husband, and he shall rule over thee.

Genesis 3:15,16

If for instance you lived in a place that was prone to earthquakes and severe thunderstorms, you would build your house a little differently. If women understood these curses properly, they would build their houses with a little more wisdom and thereby save themselves.

And I will put enmity between thee and the woman...

Genesis 3:15

Chapter 16

Why Women Must Be Spiritual

The first component of the curse is the enmity between the woman and the devil. Most of us know that the serpent was Satan. In Revelation 12:9, Satan is described as "that old serpent which deceiveth the whole world". Right here is the explanation to many of the conditions we see in the world.

Satan is the enemy of all men and of anybody who serves the Lord. However, the fact that the Lord God particularly mentioned that there would be enmity between the woman and the serpent is very significant. You will notice that this does not apply to men. If Satan is particularly against all women, this could explain why women have been targeted and destroyed all these years.

Although Satan is the enemy of all men, he is particularly the enemy of all women. This is what the Bible tells us. Satan's attacks come in different forms. This should make every woman more alert.

If the devil is particularly against women, what must women do? Every woman must take God seriously. Women must be very spiritual people who know their God. Do you think that you can fight that old serpent with your own strength? Woman, please do not deceive yourself.

Women Must Be Spiritual for Their Own Good

Every woman with direction must rise up and employ the weapons of spiritual warfare that God has placed in her hands through Christ. What folly it is when women do not take God seriously. How unfortunate when they only look to their husbands and their marriages for hope and survival.

Dear woman, except the Lord helps you, you can never defeat the devil. But with the help of God and in the name of Jesus, you can give Satan a sound thrashing!

Perhaps this is the reason why the devil keeps many women from serving the Lord. Many ladies realize that their strength for survival comes from God. Because of this there are many women who are spiritual and gravitate towards the Lord.

Yet, through marriage and related issues many of these women are cut off from effectively serving the Lord. Through one excuse or the other, many women do not amount to much in the house of the Lord.

Daughters, remember that the devil knows that he will win the fight against you once he can keep you down spiritually. Daughters, you are special targets of the devil. I didn't say it! God said it! It is his Word. But there is good news for every woman! Rise up and break through every barrier that keeps you from being the spiritual woman with direction that you were born to be.

And I will put enmity... between thy seed and her seed...

Genesis 3:15

Satan has his eye on the woman. He fears and does not understand what the seed of the woman will be and how it will affect him. Whatever that seed is, it is connected to the woman. If you were the devil, you would attack the woman so that that seed which is intended to bruise your head would never come forth. This is what is happening in the world.

There is a concerted attack by Satan on all types of women. That is why women must be spiritual. The attacks are multifaceted and multidimensional. Women almost seem to be at a disadvantage for being born into the body of a female. By the time you finish reading this book you will no longer be at a disadvantage. You will find yourself coming out of every negative situation by the wisdom of God. You will be a spiritual woman with direction!

Chapter 17

Understanding the Seed
of the Woman

Natural Seed and Spiritual Seed

Every woman will produce two types of seed or fruit. The "natural seed" and "the spiritual seed". The "natural seed" of the woman speaks of the natural children that she brings forth. The "spiritual seed" speaks of the spiritual fruit and spiritual impact of a woman's life and ministry. Every woman can have some spiritual fruit.

Since the enemy knows that the seed of the woman is what will bruise the head of the serpent, he attacks that seed all the time.

Satan Attacks the Natural Seed

The seed of the woman is a special target of Satan. The enemy does not want the woman to bring forth a child. This explains why childbearing is fraught with so many problems.

Satan wants to prevent that son or daughter from coming forth from your loins. A close look at the Bible will show you that many great men were born to women who were initially barren.

Sarah, the mother of Isaac was initially barren.

And Sarai said unto Abram, Behold now, the Lord hath restrained me from bearing: I pray thee, go in unto my maid; it may be that I may obtain children by her. And Abram hearkened to the voice of Sarai.

Genesis 16:2

Rachel who is seen as the mother of Israel, was initially barren.

And when Rachel saw that she bare Jacob no children, Rachel envied her sister; and said unto Jacob, Give me children, or else I die.

Genesis 30:1

The mother of Samson was also initially barren.

And there was a certain man of Zorah, of the family of the Danites, whose name was Manoah; and his wife was barren, and bare not.

Judges 13:2

Samuel's mother is another example of someone whose seed was under attack.

...but Hannah had no children.

1 Samuel 1:2

Elizabeth, the mother of John the Baptist, is a New Testament example of someone whose seed was blocked for many years.

And they had no child, because that Elisabeth was barren, and they both were now well stricken in years.

Luke 1:7

Woman with direction, somebody great will come out from your womb. That is why the enemy will try to hinder you from marrying or having children. If you believe in this part of the Scripture, then you will understand why demons are particularly interested in harassing women.

Satan Also Attacks the Spiritual Seed

Women are prophetically destined to make a significant spiritual impact. I have observed that the role of spiritual women has increased. More and more women are making a difference in lay ministry and full-time ministry. You cannot rule them out. Their seed is significantly impacting the work of ministry.

Women are preaching, singing, teaching and having visions. This is a role that God has carved out for all who care for spiritual things.

The Three Marys

When Mary, the sister of Martha, was seated at Jesus' feet listening to his words, he declared that she was doing the one thing needful (Luke 10:42)!

When Mary Magdalene saw the risen Christ even before the apostles, the whole church received an important message. Women are treasured by the Lord! Women are loved by the Lord! Women are special to the Saviour!

When Mary, the mother of Jesus, received her salutation from the angel, she received perhaps the most treasured words ever spoken to a woman. For the angel declared, "Hail, thou that art highly favoured, the Lord is with thee: blessed art thou among women...for thou hast found favour with God (Luke 1:28)."

These three Marys left an indelible spiritual mark that has lasted forever. That is why the name "Mary", is one of the most positive and meaningful names to be given to a woman. Their example must be followed by all who desire to bring forth spiritual seed.

A woman with direction must rise up in the realm of the spirit and refuse to be defeated. Daughter, you cannot prevent the devil from hating you. He is against your spiritual seed but it shall surely come forth!

Chapter 18

Understanding the Curse Associated with Childbearing

Unto the woman he said, I will greatly multiply thy sorrow and thy conception; in sorrow thou shalt bring forth children...

Genesis 3:16

These words you read above are the reason for the creation of the obstetric and gynaecological professions. As a medical doctor, it has always amazed me how a large profession could be created because of the female reproductive organs. We do not have large departments for treating intestines or livers. But we do have massive blocks for treating the diseases associated with the female reproductive organs.

There is such a need for a specialized department of obstetrics and gynaecology. At the Korle-Bu Teaching Hospital in Accra, Ghana, where I was trained, there are four main blocks as well as many smaller departments. One of the main blocks has to do with obstetrics and the other large department has to do with children (paediatric block).

So you can see that there are many problems associated with conception and bringing forth of children.

The female reproductive system has received much attention because of this curse.

When we are born again we are not delivered from this curse. That is an obvious reality. Women who are born again still undergo pain and sorrow in childbearing. Christ did not come to release us from the curse of Adam. All men, including Christian men still earn money by the sweat of their brows. That curse has not been lifted; you and I are still labouring under the sentence.

Some people teach that Christ has redeemed us from the curse so that when they are in labour they would have no pain or difficulty. Dear sister, do not deceive yourself and do not kill yourself. Through the wisdom of medical science, which is God-given, you can circumvent the effects of the curse. It is not a spiritual fight. It is a battle in which wisdom is a key player.

Dear woman with direction, apply the wisdom that God has made available and you will find yourself sailing through this life and having children without the curse working against you.

Christ has redeemed us from the curse of the law. There are many curses in the Bible. There are the curses of Adam and Eve, the curse of Ham, the curse on Jericho, the curse of the Law and the list goes on. Christ Jesus delivered us from the curse of the Law and not from the curse of Adam and Eve.

Christ hath redeemed us from the curse of the law, being made a curse for us: for it is written, Cursed is every one that hangeth on a tree:

Galatians 3:13

The curse of the Law can be found in Deuteronomy 28 where Moses outlines the curses that come upon those that do not keep the Law.

But it shall come to pass, if thou wilt not hearken unto the voice of the Lord thy God, to observe to do all his commandments and his statutes which I command thee this day; that all these curses shall come upon thee, and overtake thee:

Deuteronomy 28:15

Please do not make the mistake of equating the curse of the Law with the curse of Adam and Eve.

I will now share with you the key to overcoming this curse.

Chapter 19

Overcoming the Curse Associated with Childbearing

W isdom is the principal thing. Wisdom is what we need. Wisdom is the key for overcoming impossible situations. Every female problem will be solved with the wisdom of God.

Wisdom is the principal thing; therefore get wisdom: and with all thy getting get understanding. Exalt her, and she shall promote thee: she shall bring thee to honour, when thou dost embrace her.

Proverbs 4:7-8

Once again, the wisdom of God is the key to overcoming impossible situations. Medical science is God's blessing to humanity. Medical knowledge is God-given wisdom. The curse associated with childbearing can be overcome by the use of medical science.

Medical science is the application of God-given wisdom. In advanced countries, the maternal mortality rate, which is the number of deaths of women from childbearing, is less than 0.1 per 1000 total births. This means that a woman rarely dies from childbearing.

In the nineteenth century, the number of deaths of women from childbearing was alarming! It was caused mainly by things like sepsis (infections), eclampsia (high blood pressure in pregnant women), complications of labour and haemorrhage (excessive bleeding).

These complications of childbearing have been there from time immemorial. In recent times, the application of medical wisdom has changed the story of childbearing. This has largely been due to an improvement in the health and nutrition of the population. It has also been due to the control of infection, blood transfusion, advances in the fields of surgery, anaesthesia and resuscitation.

When I was a student in obstetrics and gynaecology, my professor told me that when a woman has a shoe size less than size five, she is likely to have difficulties in labour.

You see, the shoe size gives an indication of the dimensions of the pelvic bones. There must have been a whole lot of women with small shoe sizes who suffered terribly and even died in labour. But today, with the application of wisdom and modern science, women hardly need to fear childbirth. This is the principle I want you to understand. It is the same principle applied by the poor wise man who delivered the city by wisdom.

The curse of Adam presents itself as a hopeless and impossible sentence. Whenever you are faced with difficult and impossible situations never forget that wisdom can deliver you.

Wisdom is the principal thing. With all your getting, get wisdom. It will promote you and help you greatly in your life. This curse is not circumvented by using spiritual methods.

Chapter 20

Understanding the Curse Associated with Marriage

...and thy desire shall be to thy husband...
Genesis 3:16

This is an unusual curse but we see it everyday. It is not wrong for a man to desire a woman or for a woman to desire a man. However, the desire for a husband has been made into a curse because it was part of the woman's punishment for disobeying. From then on, desiring a man would be part of God's punishment for all women. In other words, the desire of women for husbands has taken on an added negative dimension. Marriage presents many frustrations to women across the globe.

It is an open secret that many married women are not happy. We can all see the troubles that married people go through. In Europe, people simply don't marry any more, they just live together.

We constantly see married couples being prayed for and counselled. Many married women are frustrated and disillusioned with the concept of marriage. There are many women who would be happier without husbands to rule over them.

Many of the nations of this world have fought for independence from foreign rule. Nobody wants to be ruled and dominated by another. "Freedom" is the reason why many wars have been fought.

People feel that they would be happier if they were free from an oppressor's rule. Yet, women do not fight for independence from men but rather fight to come under the domination of a husband! Mercy! There are many women who know that they would be more fulfilled if they remained single. Yet, there is an invisible force that makes them desire husbands. There must be a curse somewhere!

Sometimes women are unable to get these husbands. Inst
of living happy and fulfilled lives, they plod through life h
disappointed and disillusioned travellers.

...and he shall rule over thee.

Genesis 3:16

The Scripture makes it clear that the husband will rule over
the woman. This means that the woman will be dominated and
governed by the man. This is also a curse. The last line of the
national anthem of my country declares:

"And help us to resist oppressor's rule
With all our will and might forever more."

Think about it; if a whole nation is taught to "resist oppressor's
rule", then it must be a bad thing to be ruled by an oppressor.
Yet many women see oppressive men and desire to be ruled by
them. Where does this irresistible desire come from? The answer
is found in the curse pronounced in the garden of Eden.

There are many married women who have wise ideas and take
good decisions. But they are ruled and dominated by foolish
husbands. There are many men who do not exhibit the wisdom of
a ruler, yet, they occupy the place of a governor in the marriage.

It is very difficult to live with someone who does not lead
in the right direction. It is distressing to follow a leader who is
unreasonable. Yet this is the lot of many women. This also is a
curse!

Accepting that there is a curse is a first step to your victory.
Understanding how this curse plays out is key to getting your
victory. Let us now learn how to overcome this curse.

Chapter 21

Overcoming the Curse
Associated with Marriage

How does a woman come out of this apparently hopeless state of affairs? By wisdom! It is possible to overcome the desire for a husband by applying the wisdom in the Word of God.

When a woman of direction applies the wisdom of God, she will perceive marriage in the right context. I want you to see and understand what marriage can and cannot do for you.

You will have a blind desire for a husband when you don't understand what God is trying to do for you. You can be single and very happy. All women whether married or unmarried need to get this right. This is not a teaching for single people. It is a teaching for women with direction. A woman must ask herself, "What is my purpose in life?"

A Woman's Purpose

God has ordained great works for every woman. When an unmarried woman discovers that her main purpose is to accomplish the will of God, she will be content. When a married woman discovers that her main purpose in this life is to do the will of the Father, she will become a fulfilled woman.

> **For we are his workmanship, created in Christ Jesus unto good works, which God hath before ordained that we should walk in them.**
>
> **Ephesians 2:10**

Don't Look for Happiness in a Man

If you look to your husband (even Christian husbands) for fulfilment, you will not be a happy person. If you look to God for fulfilment you will be satisfied. Many married women, who have discovered this concept no longer look to their husbands for fulfilment.

I have talked with numerous single and married women. The secret to happiness for both of them is the same. Serve the Lord, give yourself to God, live for him and thereby walk in fulfilment.

Look for Happiness in God

Have you ever wondered why Jesus never considered getting married? Marriage is an arrangement that adds another dimension to life on this Earth. Jesus didn't need that dimension to be fulfilled. Jesus did not need to be married in order to be happy in this life. Jesus gave the secret to his happiness upon this Earth.

Jesus saith unto them, My meat is to do the will of him that sent me, and to finish his work.

John 4:34

Meat is the nice part of food that we all enjoy. Jesus pointed out that his enjoyment came by doing and finishing the will of God. Let's face it! How long will you live on this Earth? How many more years do you have to go before you leave this Earth?

When we get to Heaven there will be no husbands and wives.

For in the resurrection they neither marry, nor are given in marriage, but are as the angels of God in heaven.

Matthew 22:30

Will having a husband affect your future happiness in Heaven? When a woman concentrates on her real purpose for this life, she becomes a happy person.

The story of Kathryn Khulman exemplifies this principle. When Kathryn Khulman walked away from her controversial marriage that had brought much pain and disillusionment, she was able to concentrate on her ministry.

By concentrating on her ministry, as a divorced and single woman, she accomplished what many men have not been able to do. I believe she's in glory today. Do you think her being married or not matters now?

Husbands Can Quench Your Call

Many women cannot fulfil their ministries because of their husbands. One day, they will have to give an account of their ministries that never materialised. I know female pastors who have been banned by their husbands from even going to church.

Many husbands are not comfortable with their wives being so active in the ministry. Married women may seem to be elevated socially by their marital status. But one day it is women who have fulfilled their ministries who will be proud and joyful in Heaven.

I have fought a good fight, I have finished my course, I have kept the faith: Henceforth there is laid up for me a crown of righteousness...

2 Timothy 4:7, 8

This crown is laid up for women with direction! Women with direction fight a good fight and finish their course. This crown is not laid up for women because they have husbands! This crown is not given to women because they have had children! It is laid up for women who have kept the faith!

Does your marriage allow you to keep the faith? Does your marriage allow you to be a Christian? Does your marriage allow you to be in the ministry, as you would love to? Does your marriage allow you to fight and finish your course? Will you finish your course of ministry?

Come out of the curse by renewing your mind. Set your eyes on things above. Women with direction, no man (even Christian men) can give you the fulfilment I am talking about. From today let this mind be in you. The curse of desiring a man to dominate you will disappear in the name of Jesus.

When this wisdom is in you, you will be a different kind of woman. It is only by renewing your mind that you can overcome the curse!

Chapter 22

Daughter, You Have Tender Eyes

Leah was tender eyed; but Rachel was beautiful and well favoured.

Genesis 29:17

Apart from striking external beauty, there are many other things women are endowed with. It is not all about physical beauty, it is about the tenderness in the eyes.

God endows every woman with beauty or with tender eyes. God has designed some women to be tender beings. No one wants to marry a wooden pole. A man is looking for something that is warm and friendly.

Daughter, you are endowed with many other gifts. Ask any married man. "Beauty is vain," they will tell you. There are many other things that make people happy. Decide to learn the things that will make you attractive.

Because I am a pastor, I have attended many weddings. Certainly, it is not the most beautiful women who get married every Saturday! There are many beautiful girls who are sitting on the pews waiting for their turn. If it were just beauty, they would all be married by now!

God may give you beauty or he may simply give you tender eyes. Most definitely, he will give you something! Daughter, you must have something. Use what you have!

Different Kinds of Tender Eyes

Tender eyes come in many different forms. Rachel was beautiful, but Leah had tender eyes. Perhaps your tender eyes will come in the form of a friendly disposition. Perhaps your tender eyes will come as a gift of cooking and homemaking. Perhaps your tender eyes will be in the form of enchanting sexual energy. Yet still, your tender eyes may be in the form of your financial input to the marriage.

Your tender eyes may also be in the form of your exciting sanguine personality. Your tender eyes may be in the form of your cool, calm phlegmatic temperament. Yet still, your tender eyes may come in the form of your strong leader's choleric personality. Again, your melancholic neatness and loyal nature may be the tender eyes that God has given you!

Daughter, thou hast tender eyes. God gave you something. Do not be filled with self-pity. You have tender eyes. Use them and be blessed!

Chapter 23

Daughter, God Will Give
You a Husband

U ncle Laban had two daughters; both of them were eligible for
marriage. When Jacob arrived in town, he was immediately
attracted to the younger one, Rachel. But God ensured that Leah
got married before Rachel did.

> **And it came to pass in the evening, that he took Leah
> his daughter, and brought her to him; and he went
> in unto her. And Laban gave unto his daughter Leah
> Zilpah his maid for a handmaid. And it came to pass,
> that in the morning, behold, it was Leah: and he said
> to Laban, What is this thou hast done unto me? did not
> I serve with thee for Rachel? wherefore then hast thou
> beguiled me? And Laban said, It must not be so done
> in our country, to give the younger before the firstborn.**
> **Genesis 29:23-26**

Did No One Propose to You?

My sister, perhaps no one has proposed marriage to you.
You are just like our sister Leah. While other people received
proposals, you were left out. But the Lord is working on your
case.

God has a plan for you. Just as God gave Leah a husband,
God will give you a husband!

Leah married before the other so-called beautiful girls. I see
you getting married before many others. Marriage is a spiritual
thing. It is God who opens and closes the door of marriage.

> **And it came to pass in the evening, that he took
> Leah his daughter, and brought her to him; and he
> went in unto her. And Laban gave unto his daughter**

Leah Zilpah his maid for a handmaid. And it came to pass, that in the morning, behold, it was Leah: and he said to Laban, What is this thou hast done unto me? did not I serve with thee for Rachel? wherefore then hast thou beguiled me?

Genesis 29:23-25

There is a door of marriage. When it is opened to you, no one can close it! God had determined that Leah should be married. He had even determined that Leah should be married before Rachel. No one could change that blessing. Dear daughter, if God has opened the door of marriage, there is nothing that anyone can do about it.

Rachel, by popular opinion was more beautiful than her sister, and yet she did not get married before her sister. Dear daughter, you are not going to marry because of any natural reason. You are going to get married because God is holding a door open for you. Believe it and receive it in the name of Jesus!

Chapter 24

Daughter, God Will
Give You a Child

**And when the Lord saw that Leah was hated, he opened
her womb: but Rachel was barren.**

Genesis 29:31

My dear friend, have you ever watched a soccer match without
knowing who was really playing? As you watched for a while
you began to notice the side that was losing. Most of the time,
we tend to instinctively support the losing team. As they say,
"People support the underdogs."

That support you have for the underdogs is a God-given
instinct to support the disadvantaged.

Today, if you are in a disadvantaged situation, be it known
unto you that God is on your side. Woman, the Lord is helping
you right now! It may seem as though you are disfavoured, but
that is what provokes God.

The Bible says very clearly that when God saw that Leah was
not liked, he compensated for it by showing divine favour.

**And when the Lord saw that Leah was hated, he opened
her womb: but Rachel was barren.**

Genesis 29:31

God opened the womb of Leah and made her have children.
Suddenly, Leah was a favoured person. She was the only one
who could bring children into the family.

Dear sister, perhaps you are not Miss Ghana or Miss Universe.
That is the reason why Jesus is giving you extra favour. Today,
as you hold this book, remember these words, THE LORD'S
FAVOUR IS UPON YOUR LIFE!! He is going to change your
misfortunes. You don't have to be discouraged. Daughter, you
have tender eyes! Daughter, you shall surely have a child.

Chapter 25

Daughter, Keep on Serving the Lord

And she conceived again, and bare a son: and she said, Now will I praise the Lord: therefore she called his name Judah; and left bearing.

Genesis 29:35

A tender-eyed daughter is someone who continues to serve the Lord, even after God has blessed and elevated her. Leah had several children. Many people stop serving the Lord when they have children.

Leah gave birth to Reuben, Simeon, Levi and then Judah. By this time, many Christian women would have retired from their Christian activities. But not so with Leah. She said, "Now will I praise the Lord." Daughter, this is a good example to follow. You must serve the Lord with all your heart.

Children are only blessings from the Lord. My mother-in-law says that, "Children are guests in the house. They will soon be gone." If all your life is just focused on your children, you will be disappointed.

Leah determined to serve the Lord in spite of her many children.

And when the Lord saw that Leah was hated, he opened her womb: but Rachel was barren. And Leah conceived, and bare a son, and she called his name Reuben: for she said, Surely the Lord hath looked upon my affliction; now therefore my husband will love me. And she conceived again, and bare a son; and said, Because the Lord hath heard that I was hated, he hath therefore given me this son also: and she called his name Simeon. And she conceived again, and bare a son; and said, Now this time will my husband be joined

unto me, because I have born him three sons: therefore was his name called Levi. And she conceived again, and bare a son: and she said, Now will I praise the Lord: therefore she called his name Judah; and left bearing.

Genesis 29:31-35

In the midst of Leah's initial disappointment, she received four meaningful miracles. The first blessing was Reuben.

'Reuben', means 'behold'. She was saying to everyone, "See, I am blessed." She was showing everyone that God had blessed her in other ways. Count the blessings in your life. Perhaps you are not married, but you may be blessed in many other ways.

You must also say, "Reuben," which means "behold". *Behold* my good job. *Behold* my nice brothers and sisters. *Behold* my nice car. There are many things to behold.

After this, Leah had another son called Simeon. 'Simeon', means 'bearing'. In other words, 'God is sustaining me'. She was telling everyone that she could see the continued hand of God in her affairs.

Daughter of tender eyes, perhaps you do not have certain things in this life. Today, I want you to see that God is sustaining you. He is working in your life despite what you lack. You can also have a Simeon and say, "God is sustaining me."

Then Leah had a third child and called him Levi.

Levi means joined. By this time, Leah was convinced that God was a permanent part of her affairs. God was joined to her life.

She could only say thank you to the Lord for this third blessing. By naming her child Levi, she was telling everyone that God was a permanent part of her life. Woman with direction, do you have at least three blessings in your life? Perhaps things are not as perfect as you desire. But count your blessings and name them one by one: the blessings of life, the blessings of education, the blessings of health, parents, promotion and the list goes on.

Woman with direction, if you have at least three blessings in your life you can also say, "Levi." Which means God is joined to your life.

Finally, Leah had a fourth child and she called him Judah.

'Judah', means 'praise'. By naming her child Judah she was sending a message to the entire community. She was saying, "I am a happy woman." I may not be the most beautiful person. I may not be Jacob's first choice. But I can praise the Lord today.

Tender-eyed daughter, there is a miracle in your house. There is a blessing in the house. Surely you can say, "Behold God has blessed me." Surely you can say, "God is sustaining me." You must be able to say that, "God is joined to my life." Finally, you must be able to say, "Praise the Lord."

Daughter, you have tender eyes!

Chapter 26

Daughter, Don't Be Tired of Doing Your Duties

When Leah saw that she had left bearing, she took Zilpah her maid, and gave her Jacob to wife.

Genesis 30:9

L eah gave another woman to Jacob. She told her maid, "Go into his room and sleep with him." Zilpah was very willing to have an opportunity to replace her mistress.

Someone may wonder at this strange practice. However, it continues in other ways today.

Many women are welcoming a third party into their homes by their character and attitude. The Bible teaches that it is better to dwell on the rooftop than in a large house with a ferocious woman.

It is better to dwell in a corner of the housetop, than with a brawling woman in a wide house.

Proverbs 21:9

There are also many women who are not interested in sexual happiness in a Christian context. By doing this, they open the door to the numerous other women who are more than willing to be a replacement. Daughter, you may not say openly, "I want another woman to be with my husband," but by your attitude and constant accusations you are saying the same thing.

Regain Your Husband's Attention

And Reuben went in the days of wheat harvest, and found mandrakes in the field, and brought them unto his mother Leah. Then Rachel said to Leah, Give me, I pray thee, of thy son's mandrakes. And she said unto her, Is it a small matter that thou hast taken my

husband? and wouldest thou take away my son's
mandrakes also? And Rachel said, Therefore he shall
lie with thee to night for thy son's mandrakes. And
Jacob came out of the field in the evening, and Leah
went out to meet him, and said, Thou must come in
unto me; for surely I have hired thee with my son's
mandrakes. And he lay with her that night.

Genesis 30:14-16

Many years after Leah had her children, her husband was no
longer interested in her. This is a common experience in many
marriages. But it is possible to regain your husband's attention.

Woman, you are beautiful. Woman, you have tender eyes!
Daughter, there was a time you enchanted your man. If you did
it in those days you can do it again. Do not think you have lost
your ability to be a wife because you are older. Do not think that
you are no longer beautiful. Do not think that your tender eyes
are no more. In fact, with the passing of many years, your tender
eyes can be even more tender.

Leah regained her husband's attention by using her son's
mandrakes. She was a determined woman and nothing was going
to stop her from regaining her husband's attention. Woman,
I have good news for you. There is no younger girl who can
replace you. Your age and experience make you a more suitable
person for your husband. The changes in your physical features
over the years have only made you a more suitable wife.

Rise up into your place and do not allow any young
whippersnapper to intimidate you. Take your place! Pay the
price! Stop accusing, stop criticising, and stop opposing. Be
warm, energetic, youthful and interesting! Your husband will be
forever charmed with your love!

Support Your Husband

**And said unto them, I see your father's countenance,
that it is not toward me as before; but the God of my
father hath been with me. And ye know that with all**

my power I have served your father. And your father hath deceived me, and changed my wages ten times; but God suffered him not to hurt me.

If he said thus, The speckled shall be thy wages; then all the cattle bare speckled: and if he said thus, The ringstraked shall be thy hire; then bare all the cattle ringstraked. Thus God hath taken away the cattle of your father, and given them to me. And it came to pass at the time that the cattle conceived, that I lifted up mine eyes, and saw in a dream, and, behold, the rams which leaped upon the cattle were ringstraked, speckled, and grisled.

And Rachel and Leah answered and said unto him, Is there yet any portion or inheritance for us in our father's house? Are we not counted of him strangers? for he hath sold us, and hath quite devoured also our money.

For all the riches which God hath taken from our father, that is our's, and our children's: now then, whatsoever God hath said unto thee, Do.

Genesis 31:5-10,14-16

One day, there was a crisis in Jacob's life and he had to flee from his uncle. He could no longer work for his uncle's company. When it was time to leave, he told his wives about his new vision to relocate. His wives supported him. A woman with direction supports her husband when he has a new vision.

Daughter, try not to be the greatest opponent of your husband. It is true that you are the best person to correct him when he's wrong. This does not mean that you must lose your divine position as the one who supports and encourages your husband.

You must learn to balance your role as a corrector and your role as a supporter. When it is time to bring your husband into line, you must certainly do so! When it is time to support him, you must also do so wholeheartedly.

Some wives are always correcting their husbands so much that they see no good in them anymore. They can no longer receive or be led by them.

Leah had lived with her husband for many years, but when he came up with a new idea, she said unto him, "Whatever the Lord is telling you, please do it. We are with you."

Daughter you have tender eyes. Seek the wisdom of God and he will help you to do whatever you have to do!

Daughter, you have tender eyes!

Chapter 27

All about *Abigailism*

And there was a man in Maon, whose possessions were in Carmel; and the man was very great, and he had three thousand sheep, and a thousand goats: and he was shearing his sheep in Carmel. Now the name of the man was Nabal; and the name of his wife Abigail: and she was a woman of good understanding, and of a beautiful countenance: but the man was churlish and evil in his doings; and he was of the house of Caleb.

1 Samuel 25:2, 3

Abigail was a beautiful woman who was known for her role in curbing her husband's foolishness. '*Abigailism*', is the art of practising what Abigail did in order to prevent tragedy from coming to the family.

Abigail's husband was a man called Nabal. Nabal comes from the Hebrew word "qasheh", which means "foolishness or churlishness." It is translated into different words in different parts of the Bible.

Some of these are: roughly, hard, cruel, stiff-necked, stubborn, grievous, obstinate, trouble, hard-hearted and impudent.

Many married women have husbands who fit this description. A woman with direction must use wisdom to co-exist peacefully. She must use the art of *Abigailism* to have a successful marriage and combine it with a good relationship with God.

Abigailism has six goals. A woman without *Abigailism* usually achieves one or two of these goals. When you develop the art of *Abigailism* you will be able to achieve all six goals simultaneously.

Chapter 28

Six Goals of *Abigailism*

1. To prevent your husband from doing wrong or committing sin.

2. To prevent your entire family from being destroyed.

3. To preserve your marriage.

4. To preserve your relationship with God and the church.

5. To preserve your ministry.

6. To prevent a confrontation between your husband and the church.

And David heard in the wilderness that Nabal did shear his sheep. And David sent out ten young men, and David said unto the young men, Get you up to Carmel, and go to Nabal, and greet him in my name: And thus shall ye say to him that liveth in prosperity, Peace be both to thee, and peace be to thine house, and peace be unto all that thou hast. And now I have heard that thou hast shearers: now thy shepherds which were with us, we hurt them not, neither was there ought missing unto them, all the while they were in Carmel. Ask thy young men, and they will shew thee. Wherefore let the young men find favour in thine eyes: for we come in a good day: give, I pray thee, whatsoever cometh to thine hand unto thy servants, and to thy son David.

And when David's young men came, they spake to Nabal according to all those words in the name of David, and ceased. And Nabal answered David's servants, and said, Who is David? and who is the son of Jesse? there be many servants now a days that break away every man from his master. Shall I then take my bread, and my water, and my flesh that I have killed for

my shearers, and give it unto men, whom I know not whence they be?

So David's young men turned their way, and went again, and came and told him all those sayings. And David said unto his men, Gird ye on every man his sword. And they girded on every man his sword; and David also girded on his sword: and there went up after David about four hundred men; and two hundred abode by the stuff.

But one of the young men told Abigail, Nabal's wife, saying, Behold, David sent messengers out of the wilderness to salute our master; and he railed on them. But the men were very good unto us, and we were not hurt, neither missed we any thing, as long as we were conversant with them, when we were in the fields: They were a wall unto us both by night and day, all the while we were with them keeping the sheep. Now therefore know and consider what thou wilt do; for evil is determined against our master, and against all his household: for he is such a son of Belial, that a man cannot speak to him.

Then Abigail made haste, and took two hundred loaves, and two bottles of wine, and five sheep ready dressed, and five measures of parched corn, and an hundred clusters of raisins, and two hundred cakes of figs, and laid them on asses. And she said unto her servants, Go on before me; behold, I come after you. But she told not her husband Nabal.

And it was so, as she rode on the ass, that she came down by the covert of the hill, and, behold, David and his men came down against her; and she met them. Now David had said, Surely in vain have I kept all that this fellow hath in the wilderness, so that nothing was missed of all that pertained unto him: and he hath requited me evil for good. So and more also do God unto the enemies of David, if I leave of all that pertain to him by the morning light any that pisseth against the wall.

And when Abigail saw David, she hasted, and lighted off the ass, and fell before David on her face, and bowed herself to the ground, And fell at his feet, and said, Upon me, my lord, upon me let this iniquity be: and let thine handmaid, I pray thee, speak in thine audience, and hear the words of thine handmaid. Let not my lord, I pray thee, regard this man of Belial, even Nabal: for as his name is, so is he; Nabal is his name, and folly is with him: but I thine handmaid saw not the young men of my lord, whom thou didst send.

Now therefore, my lord, as the LORD liveth, and as thy soul liveth, seeing the LORD hath withholden thee from coming to shed blood, and from avenging thyself with thine own hand, now let thine enemies, and they that seek evil to my lord, be as Nabal.

And now this blessing which thine handmaid hath brought unto my lord, let it even be given unto the young men that follow my lord. I pray thee, forgive the trespass of thine handmaid: for the LORD will certainly make my lord a sure house; because my lord fighteth the battles of the LORD, and evil hath not been found in thee all thy days. Yet a man is risen to pursue thee, and to seek thy soul: but the soul of my lord shall be bound in the bundle of life with the LORD thy God; and the souls of thine enemies, them shall he sling out, as out of the middle of a sling.

And it shall come to pass, when the LORD shall have done to my lord according to all the good that he hath spoken concerning thee, and shall have appointed thee ruler over Israel; That this shall be no grief unto thee, nor offence of heart unto my lord, either that thou hast shed blood causeless, or that my lord hath avenged himself: but when the LORD shall have dealt well with my lord, then remember thine handmaid.

And David said to Abigail, Blessed be the LORD God of Israel, which sent thee this day to meet me: And blessed be thy advice, and blessed be thou, which hast kept me this day from coming to shed blood, and from avenging myself with mine own hand.

1 Samuel 25:4-33

In this passage, you see Abigail's attempt to preserve both her husband and her relationship with God's servant. It was clear that her husband was doing something wrong. You do not have to be very intelligent to see that her husband was hard-hearted and insensitive to the things of God.

Yet, she was married to him and there was no way they were going to break up. It was not the will of God for her to break up!

A daughter of destiny wants to preserve her marriage. A woman with direction also wants to preserve her ministry. Her relationship with God is very important and she is not prepared to give it up for anything. How do you balance these two when you are married to a carnal Christian or an unbeliever?

As you read these few lines, please imbibe the wisdom that comes from above and learn the strategy that Abigail adopted for the ministry.

The Bible says that there is nothing new under the sun. The types of husbands that existed in times past are the same types of husbands that you find today.

Churlishness is as prevalent today as it was in Abigail's time. That is why every woman needs the art of *Abigailism* today. There is another reason why many women need the art of *Abigailism*. This is because women are more sensitive to the things of God. They often pick up the move of the Spirit before the men do.

Abigail had heard that Samuel anointed David. She accepted immediately that he was going to be the next king.

And it shall come to pass, when the Lord shall have done to my lord according to all the good that he hath spoken concerning thee, and shall have appointed thee

ruler over Israel; That this shall be no grief unto thee, nor offence of heart unto my lord, either that thou hast shed blood causeless, or that my lord hath avenged himself: but when the Lord shall have dealt well with my lord, then remember thine handmaid.

1 Samuel 25:30,31

Perhaps there were many other people who had heard of David's anointing. Obviously, Nabal did not believe in such absurdities. He had decided to stamp out all foolish young men. He described David as a rebel. He branded him as a young, uneducated, self-appointed pastor who was chasing after people's wives. He would not allow any members of his family to attend a church that was younger than he. Does this sound familiar to you?

And Nabal answered David's servants, and said, Who is David? and who is the son of Jesse? there be many servants now a days that break away every man from his master. Shall I then take my bread, and my water, and my flesh that I have killed for my shearers, and give it unto men, whom I know not whence they be?

So David's young men turned their way, and went again, and came and told him all those sayings.

1 Samuel 25:10-12

What exactly did Abigail do? Let us take it step by step.

Chapter 29

Steps to *Abigailism*

In medical science, when you are able to make out the diagnosis of the disease you are often far advanced in curing it. If you are not able to put your finger on the exact problem, it is often difficult to solve it. You will ask yourself, "Which of these one thousand different medications should I administer to the patient?" You are still very far from the problem when you have not identified it.

1.   The first step to solving many problems is diagnosis.

First, Abigail recognized and acknowledged truthfully that she was married to a churlish personality. Acknowledging that your husband has the character and the tendencies of Nabal is the first step in the art of *Abigailism*.

Let not my lord, I pray thee, regard this man of Belial, even Nabal: for as his name is, so is he; Nabal is his name, and folly is with him: but I thine handmaid saw not the young men of my lord, whom thou didst send.

1 Samuel 25: 25

2.   The second step is to stop pretending that the problem is not there.

Many people practise what we call denial. They pretend that the problem is not there. They say that black is white and white is black. Daughter, pretending that a problem is not there does not make it go away. Calling a white thing black does not make it black.

Woe unto them that call evil good, and good evil; that put darkness for light, and light for darkness; that put bitter for sweet, and sweet for bitter!

Isaiah 5:20

There are many women who want to hide their problems. They feel that they are disgracing their husbands. There is a fine balance between denigrating your marriage, humiliating your husband and talking frankly about a problem that exists. To denigrate your husband means to blacken his reputation. This is wrong and a woman with direction does not do that!

A daughter of destiny is not so secretive that no one can help her. A certain amount of openness allows you to be helped. Dear woman, the problems that you have are not new. Read the Bible and you will realize that the problems you have are not peculiar. Speaking about your problem is not wrong if it is done in the proper context and for the right reason.

3.   **The third step of *Abigailism* is to ask for help.**

And fell at his feet, and said, Upon me, my lord, upon me let this iniquity be: and let thine handmaid, I pray thee, speak in thine audience, and hear the words of thine handmaid.

1 Samuel 25:24

Many people need help but not everybody wants it. My experience in the ministry has taught me to give help to those who ask for it and not just to those who need it. There are many needs everywhere. If you try to help some needy people, they may attack you to show their gratitude. We once experienced this when our church built a facility for a community.

Abigail asked David politely to listen to her and understand what she was going through.

4.   **The next step is to realize that God is the one who gave you your husband.**

When you are conscious of the fact that God is the one who established you in marriage, it will help you to realize that it is God who preserves the marriage.

A woman who is conscious of the fact that God brought her to where she is, never wants to be separated from the Lord.

She needs the help of the Lord in everything that she does. It is God who will keep you going.

When you have this conviction, you immediately work from God's point of view and from God's side of the fence. A woman practising *Abigailism* is on the side of the Word of God.

5. **The next step is to speak wisely to your husband.**

And Abigail came to Nabal; and, behold, he held a feast in his house, like the feast of a king; and Nabal's heart was merry within him, for he was very drunken: wherefore she told him nothing, less or more, until the morning light.

1 Samuel 25:36

The Bible says here that she told him "nothing, less or more". She did two things. First of all, she said nothing to him. It is not wise to say some things. If she had told of her donations to King David, she may have been executed that very night.

Secondly, "less or more" means in other words, she did not say anything unusual to him. Her conversation with him did not centre on the controversial issues. She told him only what he needed to know.

A fool uttereth all his mind: but a wise man keepeth it in till afterwards.

Proverbs 29:11

If you learn how to speak wisely, you will be successful at *Abigailism*. Some women quarrel with their husbands constantly. They fight about every issue and argue about every point. Men do not like arguments. Men do not like to be shouted at. Men do not like to feel they have lost an argument. No man likes to be put down. Be wise when dealing with men. *Abigailism* is the key you need. *Abigailism* means that you speak wisely to your husband.

6. **The next step is to give soft answers.**

A soft answer turneth away wrath: but grievous words stir up anger.

Proverbs 15:1

A woman practising *Abigailism* employs the weapon of soft answers. A man gravitates towards a woman with soft answers. A man yields unknowingly to a woman with soft answers. Be a woman with soft answers and you will successfully combine your marriage with your ministry.

7. **The final step is to act wisely.**

In a hopelessly difficult marriage, *Abigailism* prevails. A woman with direction is able to act so wisely that she preserves her marriage and her ministry.

In the book of Ecclesiastes, God reveals the master plan for winning in hopeless situations.

A fool also is full of words: a man cannot tell what shall be; and what shall be after him, who can tell him? The labour of the foolish wearieth every one of them, because he knoweth not how to go to the city. Woe to thee, O land, when thy king is a child, and thy princes eat in the morning!

Ecclesiastes 10:14-16

This story applies to any circumstance. It applies to a hopeless marriage, business or church. It applies to your case, in which your husband is unyielding and insensitive to the things of God. You will win in this fight because God's wisdom is the master key to overcoming impossible situations.

A wise wife does not stir up controversy with her husband. As you provide your husband with his daily requirements he will be at peace with you. If he feels that he is deprived in any way he will look for the culprit. Many Christian women unknowingly cause the church to look like the destroyer of their marriages.

Their husbands see the church and its pastors as rivals. They perceive the ministry as their enemy. Soon, the only feeling that he has for the pastor is resentment. It is sad that many husbands hate the church.

It is the duty of a woman with direction to act wisely. Do not deprive your husband of food, sex or peace at home. In fact, load it on him until he is suffocating with your love. He will be charmed by your sweetness and will have nothing to complain about.

Likewise, ye wives, be in subjection to your own husbands; that, if any obey not the word, they also may without the word be won by the conversation (behaviour) of the wives; While they behold your chaste conversation coupled with fear.

1 Peter 3:1,2

Are you married to a Nabal or to an Apostle Peter?

Coming to church must be done with great wisdom and circumspection. If you are married to someone like Nabal, you cannot afford to behave like someone who is married to Apostle Peter. Your circumstances are entirely different!

What is the result of *Abigailism*? When the art of *Abigailism* is practised, there is peace at home and peace in the Kingdom of God. Abigail prevented David's men from killing and destroying her entire household.

Many women do not realize that when their husbands are destroyed they will be destroyed as well. The mystery of marriage is that if your husband goes down, you go with him. The entire family of Abigail and Nabal would have been destroyed by David's army. Abigail would have died with her husband and children. *Abigailism* saved their lives.

Abigailism also preserved Abigail's relationship with the man of God. She was still connected to the move of God that was taking place through David. You will recall that Abigail believed in the prophecy that David was to be the next king. She was flowing with the things of the Spirit and nothing would cut her off. *Abigailism* is the key you need.

Notice David's response to Abigail. It was peaceful and there were no curses or proclamations made against her family.

And David said to Abigail, Blessed be the Lord God of Israel, which sent thee this day to meet me: And blessed be thy advice, and blessed be thou, which hast kept me this day from coming to shed blood, and from avenging myself with mine own hand.

1 Samuel 25:32,33

Nabal, on the other hand, continued in his life of foolishness and drank himself to death a few days later. You will see from the Scripture below that Abigail did not do anything to make him angry. In fact, he was so happy that he had a party. *Abigailism* does not bring about confusion and quarrels. It makes the husband so happy that he has parties!

And Abigail came to Nabal; and, behold, he held a feast in his house, like the feast of a king; and Nabal's heart was merry within him, for he was very drunken: wherefore she told him nothing, less or more, until the morning light.

1 Samuel 25:36

Apply the wisdom of God to your life and you will effectively combine your love for God with the love for your dear husband!

Chapter 30

Daughter, You Can Be Replaced!

There is a principle at work in the Earth today. It is the principle of divine displacement and replacement. This principle simply states that a person can be dislodged from a place of relative security and substituted by another unexpectedly.

You see this principle at work throughout the Bible. You see it in the life of King Saul when he was swapped for King David. You notice it in the life of Elijah the prophet. When Elijah complained about the ministry, God immediately replaced him with Elisha.

In the fifth chapter of the book of Daniel, when Belshazzar desecrated the holy vessels of the temple, a hand appeared and wrote on the wall of the king's palace. The message was simple:

...Mene; God hath numbered thy kingdom, and finished it. Tekel; Thou art weighed in the balances, and art found wanting. Peres; Thy kingdom is divided, and given to the Medes and Persians.

Daniel 5:26-28

If you do not understand biblical language, then let me explain this to you. It means that you have been substituted! These things happen before you even see them.

In soccer language, you have received a red card. You are going off the pitch! In the next match, someone else will take your place.

That is exactly what happened to Belshazzar. He was killed the very night on which the handwriting appeared. He was replaced by a man called Darius. This happened overnight.

In that night was Belshazzar the king of the Chaldeans slain. And Darius the Median took the kingdom, being about threescore and two years old.

Daniel 5:30,31

Daughter, this chapter is all about displacement and replacement. If God has exalted you and placed you in a good place, please respect it and know that you could lose your position if you do not take the Word of God seriously.

I once had to tell someone's proud wife that she should be humble because there were several people who were ready to replace her. A man of God once said, "In a congregation of five hundred there are at least twenty people who are ready to sleep with the pastor at short notice."

Wherever God has placed you, be it a political, spiritual or marital position, please be conscious of the fact that it is by the grace of God. There was a woman who was displaced and replaced swiftly in a move that shocked many observers. She was called Vashti.

Chapter 31

Daughter, Will You Obey Your Husband?

That in those days, when the king Ahasuerus sat on the throne of his kingdom, which was in Shushan the palace, In the third year of his reign, he made a feast unto all his princes and his servants; the power of Persia and Media, the nobles and princes of the provinces, being before him: When he shewed the riches of his glorious kingdom and the honour of his excellent majesty many days, even an hundred and fourscore days.

On the seventh day, when the heart of the king was merry with wine, he commanded Mehuman, Biztha, Harbona, Bigtha, and Abagtha, Zethar, and Carcas, the seven chamberlains that served in the presence of Ahasuerus the king, To bring Vashti the queen before the king with the crown royal, to shew the people and the princes her beauty: for she was fair to look on. But the queen Vashti refused to come at the king's commandment by his chamberlains: therefore was the king very wroth, and his anger burned in him.

Esther 1:2-4,10-12

Vashti was the wife of the king. She had a privileged position as the queen. Her husband asked her to do something. Perhaps the instruction was a little controversial, but I wish to use what happened to illustrate an important point. The Bible teaches that wives should submit to their own husbands.

Wives, submit yourselves unto your own husbands, as unto the Lord.

Ephesians 5:22

Because Vashti did not obey her husband, one thing led to another and she was eventually removed. Her disobedience led to a divorce. Someone may argue that her husband gave a questionable instruction that couldn't be obeyed. I agree with you. But in this case you will have to compare two bad options:

1. Humble yourself, obey this instruction and preserve your marriage or,

2. Stand up for your rights, refuse to be bullied and lose your marriage.

Which of these is a better option?

Daughter, I suggest to you that it would be wise to retain your God-given position. Do not stand up for your rights all the time. I am not saying that you should allow yourself to be maltreated. In some cases, fighting for your human rights may be more expensive than enduring moments of indignity.

Do Not Oppose Your Husband Publicly

A daughter of destiny does not oppose her husband publicly. Husband and wife may not always agree on everything. If they did, it would be a miracle. A woman may not agree with something that her husband is doing, but she will support him publicly. When they are in private she will bring up the issues and discuss her point of view. There is always a time and place to argue or discuss the issues.

The Bible teaches that the virtuous woman's husband is respected in the city. He is respected partly because of how his wife treats him.

Her husband is known in the gates, when he sitteth among the elders of the land.
Proverbs 31:23

Do Not Disgrace Your Husband

How will your husband be respected in the city if you are rude to him in public? People will think that he cannot control his own household. People will also think that he made a mistake

101

and married an "Ama Tarzan", "Ekua Rambo" or "Adjoa Terminator"!

Woman with direction, I submit to you that when your husband is disgraced, you are disgraced as well. That is one of the mysteries of the marriage covenant. When your husband goes up you go up with him. When his face is dragged in the mud, so is yours.

There are some wives who go around saying all sorts of bad things about their husbands. They have one complaint after the other. It is all right to seek help from your counsellors or pastors. But it is not all right to denigrate your husband.

"To denigrate someone," means "to blacken his reputation". Wives must not blacken the reputation of their husbands. A fine balance must be achieved between openness for obtaining advice and humiliating your husband.

Chapter 32

Daughter, Keep Your Place

Why Some Women Are Never Listened To

Wisdom is justified of her children. You can choose to oppose your husband publicly but I tell you what will happen. He will never listen to you and he will never consider your opinion in any important decision! What you do not realize is that no one takes advice from his enemy. When you constantly oppose your husband, you occupy the position of an enemy. You are the opposition party to the man.

In my observation of politics, I have noticed that the ruling party never listens to the suggestions of the opposition group. This is because the opposition group is seen as an enemy who does not have the goodwill of the ruling party at heart.

I do not listen to my enemies either. But I pay very careful attention to what my friends tell me. Have you noticed that your husband hardly listens to your antagonistic outbursts? Watch closely and notice the people he listens to. They are people he perceives as friends and genuine supporters.

Wisdom is different from human rights. It is by wisdom that hopeless marriages and difficult husbands can be turned around. God is trying to teach you wisdom and not legal rights. You have rights and claims that you can make. Please feel free to do what you want. But wisdom is justified of her children.

Do Not Allow Another to Take Your Place

Vashti was suddenly removed from her high position.

...give her royal estate unto another that is better than she.

Esther 1:19

Where has God established you? Has he made you a wife or a queen? If you do not respect what God has given you, you may lose it. I often tell people that there are two hundred people who are ready to replace them. No one needs to be proud or feel indispensable. We are all where we are by the grace of God.

Some women do not mind if their husbands are having affairs. They say, "Just do not let me know about it." Decide that you will not allow anything or anyone to take your place. A woman with direction understands the principle of divine displacement and replacement.

To bring Vashti the queen before the king with the crown royal, to shew the people and the princes her beauty: for she was fair to look on.

Esther 1:11

Vashti made a tragic mistake. She had one great asset that God had given to her, that was her physical beauty. Every woman has been given her beauty as a gift from God. You used your beauty to get the man. You must use it to keep him. You used your beauty to attract the man. You must use it to keep your place.

Some wives do not care anymore about how they look. Christian women are supposed to take care of themselves so that they look beautiful. Do not think for one moment that your husband does not notice beautiful women in town. Every Christian man is fully aware of all the beautiful women around him.

When Vashti was called upon to display her beauty, she did not! She refused to do so. Many wives do not allow their husbands to gaze upon their beautifully formed bodies. In the name of bashfulness and modesty, many Christian husbands are deprived.

Many years ago, my pastor in London told a story of a mother who was giving her daughter away in marriage. She gave her daughter one piece of advice. She said to her, "Daughter, one thing that I am proud of is that my husband, your father, has never seen my nakedness."

"Keep it that way!" she encouraged her daughter.

Woman, use your beauty to captivate your husband. Do not think that he is not interested in sexual things. The fact that he lies in the bed like a piece of dead timber does not mean that there is no sexual power within him. Unknown to you, his mind may be captivated by other women. Love is something that needs stirring and awakening.

I charge you, O daughters of Jerusalem, that ye stir not up, nor awake my love, until he please.
Song of Solomon 8:4

Christian ladies should stir up their husbands' interest with their physical beauty. I realize that many women do not believe this advice is necessary. However, as cases of adultery and divorce occur, people will take these things seriously.

The Old Man's Dog

The human body is wonderfully created by God. The power of the flesh is so strong that it must never be underestimated. In 1983, I met an old man in a little village in the north of England. This man told me that he had lost his dog. He was perturbed and mumbled on about the power of sex.

Initially, I did not understand him. He was an old man whose only friend was his dog. Eventually, I understood that his dog had deserted him and run after a female dog in the village. Being his only friend, the old man was surprised that the power of sex had been able to separate his dog from him.

All that I am saying is that sex is powerful. A daughter of destiny understands this reality. Why quarrel with someone you can charm?

Do not say that your husband is not interested; he is! Perhaps you are a proud queen like Vashti, who is not prepared to do certain things.

A proud queen will not satisfy her husband's sexual desire. A proud queen will not be prepared to have sex for any reason other than pregnancy. A proud queen will refuse all forms of sexual variations other than the basics. A proud queen will be too dignified to do anything unusual to excite her husband. A proud queen behaves like a cadaver in bed. Like a huge anaconda, she rarely moves her coiled body. She is too noble to make any movements.

Years ago, I remember a young man who gave his life to Jesus. This young man had been involved in pornography and all forms of licentiousness. His room was always covered with photographs and posters of naked women. After he got saved, he put away all these things and began to live a straight life. He got married and was faithful to his wife for many years.

When his wife became pregnant she banned him from coming near her until after she had delivered. Mind you, this was not due to medical advice. She just did not want to have sex.

After years of staying faithful, this husband turned once again to a life of lewdness and fornication. Five months into the pregnancy, he began to have affairs with other girls in his community.

His proud queen would still not hear of him coming near her until the pregnancy was over. From that time onwards, their marriage deteriorated into a cat and dog fight in which the husband had numerous extramarital affairs.

Secondary school girls took over from this twentieth century Queen Vashti.

Daughter, thou hast a body, please use it, otherwise you will be replaced!

Chapter 33

Daughter of Destiny

And we know that all things work together for good to them that love God, to them who are the called according to his purpose.

Romans 8:28

All things work together for good for a daughter of destiny. Esther had neither father nor mother. She was an orphan in the care of her cousin Mordecai. Many people would have given up on life after becoming an orphan at an early age. She could have moaned and whined that she was not receiving motherly and fatherly care at the hands of Mordecai.

Please notice the second part of the Scripture. It says that all things work together for good to them that love God. Do you love the Lord?

A woman with direction has her heart set upon the Lord. Perhaps today you are asking yourself, "Why did I marry this man?" Perhaps your life has taken many different twists and turns. You ask yourself, "Shouldn't I have married the other brother?" Your mind races as you think of missed opportunities.

I want you to know that all things work together for good. Perhaps you are well advanced in years and are not yet married. Perhaps you have been married for years and do not have a child. Perhaps you are married to a beastly husband. I tell you that all things are going to work together for good! Daughter of destiny, it is going to be well with you.

Esther had neither father, mother nor beloved. She only had a cousin. If God could raise Esther from nowhere, then God can raise you up. Daughter, I predict that it shall be well with you. He is doing it right now as you read this book.

Daughter, You Can Recover

The word 'salvation', also means 'to rescue'. Christ has rescued us from deep waters. A daughter of destiny is someone who can recover from a bad situation. All things work together for good for a daughter of destiny.

And he brought up Hadassah, that is, Esther, his uncle's daughter: for she had neither father nor mother, and the maid was fair and beautiful; whom Mordecai, when her father and mother were dead, took for his own daughter.

Esther 2:7

Esther's plight was pathetic; she had neither mother nor father. That is a serious handicap with which to begin life. But Esther recovered beautifully and rose to the highest of heights. Woman, you can recover! Some of you have been involved in all kinds of sin. Some of you have been around with countless different people. Your womb has been scraped numerous times to get rid of unwanted babies. Perhaps you were even a prostitute.

I remember speaking to some church members one day when a lady came up to me. She said, "Pastor, I don't want to ever go back to my past." As I looked at her I heard the voice of the Holy Spirit say to me, "This woman was a prostitute."

So I asked her, "What work did you do?" As she looked at me, tears welled up in her eyes and she said, "I was a prostitute." I said to her, "Daughter, you can recover! You will not go back to that life anymore."

Daughter of destiny, there is an anointing to recover. Perhaps you been used and discarded by many men. Your heart and emotions are deeply scarred from your experiences. You no longer have confidence in yourself and no longer believe in people. As he raised up Esther, he will surely raise you up.

Anyone who looked at Esther's background would never have predicted that she could be queen. She was an orphan and a refugee. How could she amount to anything? But our God is a God who specializes in making something out of nothing.

Are you nothing today? Are you a discarded rag today? Have you been disappointed and broken in this life? Let your heart be healed today because Jesus will make you a different woman. I see you recovering now!!

Woman, Listen to Advice

If Esther had not submitted herself to her cousin's suggestion to enter the beauty contest, history would have turned out differently.

...Esther was brought also unto the king's house...
Esther 2:8

A daughter of destiny submits to parental authority and to the authority of her husband. I assure you that there are no blessings outside of God's plan. If you want to be blessed, follow God's plan and you will be healed.

I have often thought that a woman's physical development outstrips her maturity. In other words, her body develops faster than her mind does.

I remember a young lady who received several proposals from several Christian brothers. She had no one to advise her. Whenever someone offered to marry her, she would laugh about it with her giggly school friends.

As the years went by, she passed the flower of her age. Suitors stopped coming and soon she realized that she had missed the opportunities of her lifetime. Many young ladies do not listen to advice at this stage of their lives. Oh, what a difference it would make if people listened to advice.

Once, such a lady came to her senses many years after the best suitors had gone by. She said to her best friend, "I have really made a big mistake. I wish I had married so-and-so." I can remember advising this young lady in particular. She got so angry with me that she would not have anything to do with me after that.

Up until this day, I can hardly maintain a conversation with her. She was so averse to my suggestions and advice in her younger days. As this lady approaches her menopause, she is still unmarried. Zimbo!* A little wisdom makes a lot of difference to a woman's life. I sometimes look at the brother who would have married her and say to myself, "My stubborn friend missed a good chance."

...wisdom is profitable to direct.

Ecclesiastes 10:10

Daughter of destiny, be submissive and listen to advice. Do not become an old and lonely woman before you admit that you were wrong. Do not wait for your marriage to break up before you believe the advice you have received. I personally think that some people want bad things to happen before they submit to the Word of God.

Woman, Nothing Happens by Chance!

...and who knoweth whether thou art come to the kingdom for such a time as this?

Esther 4:14

A Daughter Must Help Her Father

The years went by and Esther was established as the queen of the land. But trouble brewed and soon Esther was called upon to help. Her cousin reminded her of how she was in a privileged position. He told her, "Perhaps there is a reason why you are here. Perhaps this is why God allowed you to be elevated to this lofty position."

---

* The expression "Zimbo" is the author's colloquial exclamation.

A daughter of destiny will not quickly forget where she came from. She is prepared to help her father. Esther helped Mordecai. A daughter of destiny will remember her father and help him.

Esther may never have known what it cost Mordecai to care for her. Daughter, help your fathers in the natural! Daughter, help your spiritual father! Remember him and remember all that he has done for you. Don't forget what he has done for you. Perhaps, you will never know the price he paid to care for you.

This is a wonderful poem from a daughter to her father. Perhaps you could write these words to your father.

> *Dad, as I was growing up,*
> *You always made my world feel safe.*
> *The dear calm of your voice, calmed me...*
> *And the strong circle of your arms circled me.*
> *I never felt vulnerable or afraid,*
> *Because to me, you seemed unshakable.*
> *As I got older, though,*
> *It dawned on me that the world you faced everyday*
> *Was a lot bigger and scarier*
> *Than the one you had created for me.*
> *And I wondered, sometimes, if you felt*
> *Like relying on someone else's strength for a change...*
> *Now that I am an adult and living on*
> *The outside of your safety net,*
> *I finally understand what sacrifices*
> *You made to make sure "my world"*
> *Felt alright all the time.*
> *Growing up in the sanctuary of your love*
> *Is something*
> *I will always cherish and a memory*
> *I could never forget.*

Dierdra J. Brown

I am sometimes amazed that people who have lived with others and at the expense of relatives all their lives, would not like to help anyone in later years. They close the doors to other needy people. They forget what someone did for them.

A virtuous woman has a kind heart. She is generous and helps many people, even those who do not deserve it.

She stretcheth out her hand to the poor; yea, she reacheth forth her hands to the needy.

Proverbs 31:20

Perhaps you are the wife of some important personality today. Perhaps you are living in a rich western nation. Nothing happens by chance. Esther was not a beautiful woman by chance. Her parents did not die by chance. If her parents had been alive, they might not have put her up for the beauty contest.

Perhaps you are occupying a position in which you can employ many Christians. Please note that it is for a reason. God is the one who established you wherever you are. He will come knocking at your door to ask you for your help. Will you help the cause of the gospel when it is your turn to do so, or will you find an excuse?

Daughter, God Comes before Marriage!

Esther sent an important message back to Mordecai. She explained that it would not be possible for her to walk into the king's parlour without being invited. She explained that she would lose her life if she did so.

Go, gather together all the Jews that are present in Shushan, and fast ye for me, and neither eat nor drink three days, night or day: I also and my maidens will fast likewise; and so will I go in unto the king, which is not according to the law: and if I perish, I perish

Esther 4:16

112

But Esther put God before her marriage. She obeyed the Word of God. She was prepared to sacrifice her life if that was what it meant. She remembered where she came from.

How many women would be prepared to make such a sacrifice for a religious cause? Esther risked everything! If you put God first you will invoke a blessing upon your life.

Daughter, Fast and Pray!

Esther asked the people to fast and pray. She believed that prayer and fasting would bring solutions. Daughter of destiny, in all your getting, get prayer and fasting. Perhaps, no one can change your husband's mind. But I know one thing that can help to break every barrier down – prayer and fasting.

Then Esther bade them return Mordecai this answer, Go, gather together all the Jews that are present in Shushan, and fast ye for me, and neither eat nor drink three days, night or day: I also and my maidens will fast likewise; and so will I go in unto the king, which is not according to the law: and if I perish, I perish.
Esther 4:15,16

Esther did not just ask her followers to fast, she told them that she would fast herself. If you want to be a daughter of destiny, learn these principles today.

Your destiny is determined more by prayer than anything else. Jesus determined his destiny by prayer. Three hours of prayer in the garden of Gethsemane ensured that everything would go as planned.

Become a daughter of destiny. Shape your marriage through prayer. Carve out your future with hours of prayer. Pray in the day, pray in the night. Pray all the time. Daughter of destiny, pray without ceasing!